ROMEO AND JULIET

William Shakespeare

PEACOCK BOOKS

Published by
PEACOCK BOOKS
7/22, Ansari Road, Darya Ganj, New Delhi-110002
Phones : +91-11-40775252, 40775214, 23273880, 23275880
Fax : +91-11-23285873
Web : www.atlanticbooks.com
E-mail : orders@atlanticbooks.com

Peacock Books is an imprint of
Atlantic Publishers and Distributors (P) Ltd

First published 1597

Printed & bound in India by Atlantic Print Services

CONTENTS

SHAKESPEARE'S PLAYS WITH THEIR PROBABLE APPROXIMATE DATES

There is absence of total agreement on the dates of Shakespearean plays. Some scholars give an earlier date than the one suggested here for Shakespeare's first play. Doubt also remains concerning the actual order of composition in particular years. Having stated that, the editor gives hereunder the approximate dates as largely accepted by Shakespeare scholars in general.

1590-91

Henry VI Part II
Henry VI Part III

1591-92

Henry VI Part I

1592-93

Richard III
Comedy of Errors

1593-94

Titus Andronicus
Taming of the Shrew

1594-95

Two Gentlemen of Verona
Love's Labour's Lost
Romeo and Juliet

1595-96

Richard II
Midsummer Night's Dream

1596-97

King John
Merchant of Venice

1597-98

Henry IV Part I
Henry IV Part II

1598-99

Much Ado About Nothing
Henry V

1599-1600

Julius Caesar
As You Like It
Twelfth Night

1600-1601
Hamlet
Merry Wives of Windsor

1601-02
Troilus and Cressida

1602-03
All's Well That Ends Well

1604-05
Measure for Measure
Othello

1605-06
King Lear
Macbeth

1606-07
Antony and Cleopatra

1607-08
Coriolanus
Timon of Athens

1608-09
Pericles

1609-10
Cymbeline

1610-11
Winter's Tale

1611-12
The Tempest

1612-13
Henry VIII
Two Noble Kinsmen

WILLIAM SHAKESPEARE
Biographical Sketch

1. A Symbol of Culture

Introducing Shakespeare to the general reader, G.B. Harrison begins his book with the following statement:

> No household in the English-speaking world is properly furnished unless it contains copies of the *Holy Bible* and of *The Works of William Shakespeare*. It is not always thought necessary that these books should be read in maturer years, but they must be present as symbols of Religion and Culture.

Not only in the English speaking world, but everywhere, acquaintance with Shakespeare's plays is regarded as a mark of culture; and there is hardly any language-community in the civilized world, which does not possess Shakespeare in translation.

2. Life

Anyone looking for reliable historical information about Shakespeare is bound to meet with disappointment. We get very little help from his contemporaries in the form of recorded reference allusion, or memoirs, Shakespeare himself is completely silent about himself, and as regards his works, he has consumed himself into them so perfectly that it is very risky to draw any clear inferences from his works—except, perhaps, the sonnets, some of which, departing from the convention, appear to be expressing personal experience. We do, however, get some definite information from the parish register, legal documents and town records.

At first sight, it may appear astonishing that such a great writer as Shakespeare should have received no notice from his contemporaries and that no attempt should have been made to preserve every bit of the records associated with his life. But a second look at the state of affairs and attitude to biography prevailing in that period will mollify our uneasiness. The Elizabethans, generally, were indifferent to biographical and autobiographical notes and memoirs; even the biography of the most important personage, Queen Elizabeth herself, is full of gaps and guesses. It should, in fact, be gratifying that we possess more of authentic information about Shakespeare than about any of his contemporary writers excepting Ben Jonson. Moreover, Shakespeare, until very late in his life, was a very ordinary individual belonging to the socially unwelcome profession of actor; and the playwrights, too, were not much distinguished in the society. The critical response to his work was not unmixed high praise until the end of the eighteenth century. It was only in the beginning of the nineteenth century that Shakespeare became established as a great writer who must be spoken of with a feeling of reverence. But during the intervening centuries, he had been steadily moving towards the highest position, and as this process advanced, his admirers became over enthusiastic to complete his biography. The result was an infusion of a great deal of guesswork aggrandisement and romanticising. In such a situation, the best policy will be to keep close to the attested facts and reasonable inferences, except in cases where a highly dubious anecdote may, nevertheless, indicate some important turn in the dramatist's life.

William Shakespeare—the surname is found spelled in various other ways, which was not unusual in those days—was the son of John Shakespeare of Stratford-on-Avon. In 1556

John Shakespeare bought a house in Henley Street. In 1552, he, along with two neighbours, had been fined for keeping an unauthorized dunghill on Henley Street, which means he had been dwelling there for some years before he bought the house. In 1557 he married Mary Arden, the daughter of Robert Arden, a land-owning farmer who lived in Wilmcote, a small village two miles from Stratford. Mary brought with her an inheritance of sixty acres of land.

John Shakespeare was a glove-maker and dealer in wool, he may have at one time or another, pursued some other trades as well. He was a prosperous citizen of Stratford and one of its notables.

In the year of William Shakespeare's birth, however, his father was a prosperous businessman who was also a man of substance and of social standing. William, the third and surviving child of John and Mary Shakespeare was baptized on 26 April 1564. Allowing the usual period of three days between birth and baptism, it is generally assumed that William Shakespeare was born on 23 April 1564, which is also the day of the feast of St. George, the patron saint of England—and this is also the day on which Shakespeare breathed his last. The Shakespeares had five more children. It requires no documentary evidence to say that Shakespeare during his childhood observed and absorbed the life of town and village surging all around him and, possessing a rare talent, he stored in his mind sights, sounds, scenes and characters, which, combined with his experience of London, would prove a rich material at the forge of his creativity, when he came to write poems and plays.

There is no valid reason to doubt that William was enrolled in the local grammar school when he was six or seven years old. His father was still a prominent citizen and an important member of the borough council. But the school records for the period are not available. Nicholas Rowe, who brought out the first edited collection of Shakespeare's plays, wrote in his introduction that the boy studied in a free school where "it is probable, he acquired what Latin he was master of, but the narrowness of his circumstances, and the want of his assistance at home, forced his father to withdraw him from thence, and unhappily prevented his further proficiency in that language". John Aubrey a seventeenth-century antiquarian and biographer, in his *Brief Lives* published posthumously in 1813, informs us that Shakespeare had been a school master in a country school.

There is, however, no confusion regarding his early marriage to Anne Hathaway, who was about eight years his senior. One thing that can be safely inferred is that Shakespeare was an impetuous and highly romantic young man and this conclusion gets ample support in the essential nature of all his writings—they are romantic through and through. On 26th May 1583, their first issue Susanna was baptized in Stratford and two years later, the twins, Hamnet and Judith were born and christened on 2 February 1585. Of these children of Shakespeare, Hamnet died in 1596, Susanna married a physician named John Hall and inherited a major portion of her father's assets, Judith married Thomas Quiney.

The period from 1585 to 1592 in Shakespeare's life is known as the "dark years" or "lost years" from the biographer's point of view. For this period we have no authentic information about the family apart from a single reference to John Shakespeare in 1588 in connection with a legal dispute over a sum of money. There is, however, no dearth of legend and hearsay. According to Nicholas Rowe, Shakespeare incurred the wrath of the local landlord, Sir Thomas Lucy for stealing deer in his park and was, as a result, obliged to flee to London.

Though there are many conjectures, yet what sounds most credible is that Shakespeare attached himself to one of the touring theatrical companies that visited the countryside during the period under consideration. Three such companies, the Earl of Worcester's Men, the Earl of Oxford's Men and the Earl of Essex's Men, were giving performances at Stratford in 1581 and in 1585 the town people were entertained by an unidentified company. In 1587, the year in which Shakespeare most probably left his home town, the Earl of Essex's Men and the Earl of Leicester's Men were in Stratford; he might have accompanied one of these groups to London.

In the midst of financial and other problems besetting the family, joining a company of actors must have appealed to Shakespeare as a good expedient because it would bring some wages as well as give him an access to the literary world of London.

By 1592 Shakespeare's struggle had begun to bear fruit; in that year he was worthy enough to arouse the jealousy of another playwright, Robert Greene, one of the University Wits. In a letter addressed to his fellow writers and appended to a pamphlet called *Greene's Groatsworth of Wit Bought with a Million of Repentance* he made a scurrilous attack on Shakespeare for presuming to be not only an actor but the best playwright.

It is clear that by 1592 Shakespeare had established himself in London as an actor and dramatist: he had completed at least the three plays comprising the *Henry VI* trilogy; he had also probably been improving and retouching existing plays and there might have been some talk of his writing then in progress. Some scholars have argued that he had also completed or was about to complete *The Two Gentlemen of Verona, The Comedy of Errors, The Taming of the Shrew, Richard III, Titus Andronicus* and *Love's Labour's Lost.*

The next year, 1593, saw the publication of a long narrative poem, *Venus and Adonis,* with a signed dedication to Henry Wriothesley, the third Earl of Southampton: Your Honour's in all duty, William Shakespeare." In the following year came out another poem, *The Rape of Lucrece,* also dedicated to the same lord. This was the period during which the London theatres remained closed on account of the plague; that Shakespeare did not waste his time, but was busy writing poetry shows with what earnestness he pursued his aim of achieving literary renown. He had also started writing his sonnets during this period and some scholars have suggested that the group of sonnets addressed to a young man had the Earl of Southampton for their inspirator.

The theatres reopened in 1594 and staging of plays including some by Shakespeare began. We find that he is already an important member of Lord Chamberlain's company as disclosed by the following entry in the Chamber Accounts:

> To William Kemp, William Shakespeare, and Richard Burbage, servants to the Lord Chamberlain, upon the Council's warrant dated at Whitehall 15 March 1594 (-5) for two several comedies or interludes showed by them before her Majesty in Christmas time last past, *viz.* upon St. Stephen's day and Innocent's day, £ 13 6s, 8d, and by way of her Majesty's reward £ 6 13s, 4d.

From recorded references, allusions and lists of actors prefixed to printed plays, we gather that Shakespeare continued to act on the stage at least up to 1603 and if we rely on his fellow-actors, John Heminge and Henry Condell, who edited the First Folio edition of his plays in 1623, up to 1611. He is said to have played kingly roles including the Ghost in *Hamlet* but he also acted the part of old servant Adam in *As You Like It*. According to Aubrey, he "did act exceedingly well".

All the while Shakespeare was making steady progress in writing plays and in earning money and fame. During 1595-96, five of his new plays were produced: *Richard II, Romeo and Juliet, King John, A Midsummer Night's Dream,* and *The Merchant of Venice*. During the latter year there was a tragedy in the family: his only son Hamnet died in August 1596. In the same year, there was some more trouble for Shakespeare: according to a reference discovered by Leslie Hotson in 1931, one William Wayt claimed sureties of the peace against William Shakespeare and some other persons including Francis Langley then owner of the Swan Theatre. But his financial position was quite sound. He was living in a large house in Bishopsgate as the tax-rolls indicate, perhaps his family also stayed with him for brief periods. There is evidence of his purchase of property in London and in his hometown.

While living in London, Shakespeare appears to have maintained good links with his native place and its people. His narrative poems had been printed by Richard Field who had migrated from Stratford. In 1597 Shakespeare bought the largest house in Stratford, called New Place, from William Underhill for a sum of £ 60. On October 25, 1598, Richard Quiney a Stratford man who was visiting London wrote a letter to Shakespeare requesting a loan of £ 30. In 1599 the famous actor, Richard Burbage and his brother Cuthbert set up a new playhouse on the Bankside, called the Globe. Since they could not finance the project on their own, they invited some other members of their company, Lord Chamberlain's Men, to become shareholders. Shakespeare thus became a part-owner of the Globe, entitled to ten per cent of the profits. He enjoyed the unique privilege of being a dramatist, actor and businessman.

During the period 1597-99 six more plays comprising comedies and plays on English history were produced:
Merry Wives of Windsor, Much Ado About Nothing, As You Like It, Henry IV-Part One, Henry IV-Part Two, and *Henry V*, probably *Julius Caesar* also had its first staging in 1599.

The new century opened with a personal tragedy to Shakespeare: his father died in 1601. It also brought him to the threshold of his tragic vision—the truest and profoundest ever presented to theatre audiences and to the readers of the world. Before the death of Queen Elizabeth in 1603, the greatest tragedy of personal dilemma *Hamlet* had its first performance. His finest comedy, *Twelfth Night* and the 'problem play' *Troilus and Cressida* were also produced before 1603. With the accession of King James to the English throne, Lord Chamberlain's Men, evidently regarded as the best company of actors, was taken under royal patronage and was renamed King's Men. The letters patent issued on 19 May 1603 mention William Shakespeare along with some other members of the company including Heminge and Condell, the future editors of the first edition of his Collected Plays. The actors of the company became eligible to special privileges; records indicate that they were often called upon to present plays before the Court and to participate in royal pageants and processions—several Shakespeare plays were performed at the Court. In March 1604, when King James made a 'royal proceeding' through the city of London, Shakespeare—as well as each of his fellow players—was given four yards of red cloth for his livery.

On the plane of worldly affairs too, Shakespeare was faring very well. In may 1602 he purchased one hundred and seven acres of arable land to the parish of old Stratford and in September he acquired a cottage in Chapel Lane, Stratford-on-Avon. A fellow actor, Augustine Phillipps, when he made his will in May 1605, mentioned Shakespeare first among the recipients of his bequests of gold pieces: "I give and bequeath to my fellow, William Shakespeare, a thirty-shilling piece in gold." Two years later in 1607 his favourite daughter Susanna, married the physician John Hall and in February 1608 their daughter Elizabeth was born. It is almost certain that Edmond Shakespeare whose burial is recorded in the registers of the Church of St. Saviours in Southwark was the poet's brother. Shakespeare's mother died in 1608.

In Shakespeare's literary output, the period 1604-1608 is the period of great tragedies: *Othello, Macbeth, King Lear, Antony and Cleopatra* and *Cariolanus*. The other plays first produced during this period are: *Measure for Measure, All is Well That Ends Well* and *Timon of Athens*. Some scholars, however, believe that *All's Well That Ends Well* is an early play, perhaps *Love's Labour's Won*, mentioned by Francis Meres in his *Palladis Tamia* (1598).

In 1608 the King's Men took over the Blackfriars, an indoor theatre where Henry Evans's children's company had been staging plays since 1600. Shakespeare thus began writing plays for both Blackfriars and the Globe. He appears to have adjusted himself to the conditions and upper-class audiences at the Blackfriars. Otherwise, too, Shakespeare about this time had emerged from the Inferno of human and supernatural evil. He had explored the genesis, nature, working and consequences of evil and expressed them in the best of utterance. Now in the last phase of his career, he turned to superior kinds of solutions. Evil keeps raising its head, but it is confronted by higher human nature and is overthrown without waste or destruction. This is the tenor of his last plays: *Pericles, Cymbeline, The Winter's Tale, The Tempest.*

William Shakespeare had made his life a grand success: Whatever wrongs, malice, envy or injury he had suffered were behind him; he had become rich and respected; thousands of human hearts had been moved to laughter and tears by the magic of his lines; he had learnt the last lesson in human wisdom.

Around 1611 Shakespeare contentedly retired to Stratford. His remaining two younger brothers, Gilbert and Richard died in 1612 and 1613 respectively. John Combe, one of his closest friends also died in 1613 leaving him a bequest of £ 5. On March 10, 1613, he bought the Blackfriar's Gate House.

Shakespeare did not break his relations completely with his company; he also kept visiting London from time to time. The last two plays which he wrote in collaboration with John Fletcher are *Henry VII* and *The Two Noble Kinsmen*, but his heart wasn't there; they suffer in execution and in imaginative power. Shakespeare's health began to deteriorate after 1613. According to one report some time in 1616 Drayton and Ben Jonson came down to visit him and they had a merry meeting. His will was drawn up in January 1616. Since his younger daughter Judith got married to Thomas Quiney on February 10, the will was revised and executed by him on March 25.

In his will, Shakespeare bequeathed nearly all his property to his elder daughter Susanna Hall and her husband; Judith his younger daughter received very little in comparison. Perhaps Shakespeare was not happy with Judith's marriage to Thomas Quiney about whom there was some scandal, or, he feared any fixed assets made over to her would not remain secure, but he made provision for yearly payment of some money to her. This apparent lack of balance on the part of Shakespeare is bound to remind us of his own creation *King Lear*.

Another matter which causes surprise is the bequest to his wife. She is not mentioned by name and Shakespeare appears to have added one sentence about her as an after thought: "I give unto my wife my second best bed with the furniture". Those who defend Shakespeare on this issue argue that the best bed in the house would be reserved for guests, that he gave her the second best bed because it carried past associations since this must have been the bed the couple used to sleep in. It is also true that Anne's dower rights already stood protected by law; she must have continued to live in New Place until her death in 1623. And yet, when all this has been said, one cannot help feeling that this slighting gesture on the part of Shakespeare indicates that something had gone sour in their relations.

He left something to each of his relations: niece Elizabeth Hall, sister Joan and her three sons; he did not forget his friends and the poor of Stratford, to whom he bequeathed ten pounds. It is to be noted that he gave 26s. 8d. each to his former fellow actors, John Heminge, Richard Burbage and Henry Condell for buying mourning rings.

Shakespeare died on 23 April, 1616, but Death could not be proud of this, for in black ink his name still shines bright. A monument representing the poet in the act of writing with a quill was installed some time between his death and the year 1623. This is the famous bust with which the whole world has become familiar. The other authentic likeness is Martin Droeshout's engraving on the title page of the First Folio Collection of Shakespeare's Plays, which is equally familiar to readers. The epitaph inscribed under the bust praises Shakespeare as a writer.

With whome
Quick nature died; whose name doth deck
this tombe
Far more than most, sith all that He hath writt
Leaves living art, but page, to serve his witt.

The Most Excellent and Lamentable Tragedy of Romeo and Juliet

ROMEO AND JULIET

DRAMATIS PERSONÆ

ESCALUS, CHORUS, *Prince of Verona*
PARIS, *a young nobleman, kinsman to the Prince*
MONTAGUE and CAPULET, *heads of two houses at variance with each other*
An Old Man, *of the Capulet family*
ROMEO, *son to Montague*
MERCUTIO, *Kinsman to the Prince, and friend to Romeo*
BENVOLIO, *nephew to Montague, and friend to Romeo*
TYBALT, *nephew to Lady Capulet*
FRIAR LAWRENCE, FRIAR JOHN , *a Franciscans*
BALTHASAR, *servant to Romeo*
SAMPSON, & GREGORY, *servants to Capulet*
PETER, *Servant to Juliet's nurse*
ABRAHAM, *servant to Montague*
An Apothecary
Three Musicians
An Officer
LADY MONTAGUE, *wife to Montague*
LADY CAPULET, *wife to Capulet*
JULIET, *daughter to Capulet*
Nurse *to Juliet*
Citizens of Verona; Gentlemen and Gentlewoman of both Houses; Maskers, Torchbearers, Pages, Guards, Watchmen, Servants, and Attendants

THE SCENE: *Verona and Mantua*

THE PROLOGUE

Enter CHORUS

Two households, both alike in dignity,
In fair Verona, where we lay our scene,
From ancient grudge break to new mutiny,
Where civil blood makes civil hands unclean.
From forth the fatal loins of these two foes
A pair of star-cross'd lovers take their life;
Whose misadventured piteous overthrows
Doth with their death bury their parents' strife.
The fearful passage of their death-mark'd love,
And the continuance of their parents' rage,
Which, but their children's end, nought could remove,
Is now the two hours' traffic of our stage;
The which if you with patient ears attend,
What here shall miss, our toil shall strive to mend.

Exit

Act I

Scene I—*Verona: A public place*

Enter SAMPSON and GREGORY, of the house of Capulet, with swords and bucklers on

SAMPSON: Gregory, o' my word, we'll not carry coals.

GREGORY: No, for then we should be colliers.

SAMPSON: I mean, an we be in choler, we'll draw.

GREGORY: Ay, while you live, draw your neck out o' collar.

SAMPSON: I strike quickly, being moved.

GREGORY: But thou art not quickly moved to strike.

SAMPSON: A dog of the house of Montague moves me.

GREGORY: To move is to stir, and to be valiant is to stand; therefore, if thou art moved, thou runn'st away.

SAMPSON: A dog of that house shall move me to stand. I will take the wall of any man or maid of Montague's.

GREGORY: That shows thee a weak slave; for the weakest goes to the wall.

SAMPSON: 'Tis True; and therefore women, being the weaker vessels, are ever thrust to the wall; therefore I will push Montague's men from the wall and thrust his maids to the wall.

GREGORY: The quarrel is between our masters and us their men.

SAMPSON: 'Tis all one; I will show myself a tyrant. When I have fought with the men, I will be civil with the maids—I will cut off their heads.

GREGORY: The heads of the maids?

SAMPSON: Ay, the heads of the maids, or their maidenheads; take it in what sense thou wilt.

GREGORY: They must take it in sense that feel it.

SAMPSON: Me they shall feel while I am able to stand, and; 'tis known I am a pretty piece of flesh.
GREGORY: 'Tis well thou art not fish; if thou hadst, thou hadst been poor-John. Draw thy tool; here comes two of the house of the Montagues.

Enter two other Servingmen, ABRAHAM and BALTHASAR

SAMPSON: My naked weapon is out; quarrel, I will back thee.
GREGORY: How? turn thy back and run?
SAMPSON: Fear me not.
GREGORY: No, marry; I fear thee!
SAMPSON: Let us take the law of our sides; let them begin.
GREGORY: I will frown as I pass by, and let them take it as they list.
SAMPSON: Nay, as they dare. I will bite my thumb at them, which is disgrace to them if they bear it.
ABRAHAM: Do you bite your thumb at us, sir?
SAMPSON: I do bite my thumb, sir.
ABRAHAM: Do you bite your thumb at us, sir?
SAMPSON: [*Aside to Gregory*] Is the law of our side, if I say ay?
GREGORY: [*Aside to Sampson*] No.
SAMPSON: No, sir, I do not bite my thumb at you, sir; but I bite my thumb, sir.
GREGORY: Do you quarrel, sir?
ABRAHAM: Quarrel sir! No, sir.
SAMPSON: But if you do, sir, I am for you. I serve as good a man as you.
ABRAHAM: No better?
SAMPSON: Well, sir.

Enter BENVOLIO

GREGORY: [*Aside to Sampson*] Say 'better'; here comes one of my master's kinsmen.
SAMPSON: Yes, better, sir.

ABRAHAM: You lie.

SAMPSON: Draw, if you be men. Gregory, remember thy swashing blow.

They fight

BENVOLIO: Part, fools!

Beats down their swords

Put up your swords; you know not what you do.

Enter TYBALT

TYBALT: What, art thou drawn among these heartless hinds?
Turn thee, Benvolio; look upon thy death.

BENVOLIO: I do but keep the peace; put up thy sword,
Or manage it to part these men with me.

TYBALT: What, drawn, and talk of peace! I hate the word,
As I hate hell, all Montagues, and thee.
Have at thee, coward!

They fight

Enter an Officer, and three or four Citizens with clubs or partisans

OFFICER: Clubs, bills, and partisans! Strike; beat them down.

CITIZEN: Down with the Capulets! Down with the Montagues!

Enter Old CAPULET in his gown, and his Wife

CAPULET: What noise is this? Give me my long sword, ho!

LADY CAPULET: A crutch, a crutch! Why call you for a sword?

CAPULET: My sword, I say! Old Montague is come,
And flourishes his blade in spite of me.

Enter Old MONTAGUE and his Wife

MONTAGUE: Thou villain Capulet!—Hold me not, let me go.

LADY MONTAGUE: Thou shalt not stir one foot to seek a foe.

Enter PRINCE ESCALUS, with his Train

PRINCE: Rebellious subjects, enemies to peace,

Profaners of this neighbour-stained steel—
Will they not hear? What, ho! you men, you beasts,
That quench the fire of your pernicious rage
With purple fountains issuing from your veins!
On pain of torture, from those bloody hands
Throw your mistemper'd weapons to the ground,
And hear the sentence of your moved prince.
Three civil brawls, bred of an airy word,
By thee, old Capulet, and Montague,
Have thrice disturb'd the quiet of our streets
And made Verona's ancient citizens
Cast by their grave beseeming ornaments
To wield old partisans, in hands as old,
Canker'd with peace, to part your canker'd hate.
If ever you disturb our streets again,
Your lives shall pay the forfeit of the peace.
For this time all the rest depart away.
You, Capulet, shall go along with me;
And, Montague, come you this afternoon,
To know our farther pleasure in this case,
To old Free-town, our common judgment-place.
Once more, on pain of death, all men depart.

Exeunt all but MONTAGUE, his Wife, and BENVOLIO

MONTAGUE: Who set this ancient quarrel new abroach?
Speak, nephew; were you by when it began?

BENVOLIO: Here were the servants of your adversary
And yours, close fighting ere I did approach.
I drew to part them; in the instant came
The fiery Tybalt, with his sword prepared;
Which, as he breathed defiance to my ears,
He swung about his head and cut the winds,
Who, nothing hurt withal, hiss'd him in scorn.

While we were interchanging thrusts and blows,
Came more and more, and fought on part and part.
Till the Prince came, who parted either parts.

LADY MONTAGUE: O, where is Romeo? Saw you him to-day?
Right glad I am he was not at this fray.

BENVOLIO: Madam, an hour before the worshipp'd sun
Peer'd forth the golden window of the east,
A troubled mind drew me to walk abroad;
Where, underneath the grove of sycamore
That westward rooteth from the city's side,
So early walking did I see your son.
Towards him I made; but he was ware of me
And stole into the covert of the wood.
I, measuring his affections by my own,
Which then most sought where most might not be found,
Being, one too many by my weary self,
Pursued my humour, not pursuing his,
And gladly shunn'd who gladly fled from me.

MONTAGUE: Many a morning hath he there been seen,
With tears augmenting the fresh morning's dew,
Adding to clouds more clouds with his deep sighs;
But all so soon as the all-cheering sun
Should in the farthest east begin to draw
The shady curtains from Aurora's bed,
Away from the light steals home my heavy son,
And private in his chamber pens himself,
Shuts up his windows, locks far daylight out,
And makes himself an artificial night.
Black and portentous must this humour prove,
Unless good counsel may the cause remove.

BENVOLIO: My noble uncle, do you know the cause?

MONTAGUE: I neither know it nor can learn of him.
BENVOLIO: Have you importuned him by any means?
MONTAGUE: Both by myself and many other friends.
But he, his own affections' counsellor,
Is to himself—I will not say how true;
But to himself so secret and so close,
So far from sounding and discovery,
As is the bud bit with an envious worm,
Ere he can spread his sweet leaves to the air,
Or dedicate his beauty to the sun.
Could we but learn from whence his sorrows grow,
We would as willingly give cure as know.

Enter ROMEO

BENVOLIO: See where he comes. So please you step aside;
I'll know his grievance or be much denied.
MONTAGUE: I would thou wert so happy by thy stay
To hear true shrift. Come, madam, let's away.

Exeunt MONTAGUE and his Wife

BENVOLIO: Good morrow, cousin.
ROMEO: Is the day so young?
BENVOLIO: But new struck nine.
ROMEO: Ay me! sad hours seem long.
Was that my father that went hence so fast?
BENVOLIO: It was. What sadness lengthens Romeo's hours?
ROMEO: Not having that which having makes them short.
BENVOLIO: In love?
ROMEO: Out—
BENVOLIO: Of love?
ROMEO: Out of her favour where I am in love.
BENVOLIO: Alas that love, so gentle in his view,
Should be so tyrannous and rough in proof!
ROMEO: Alas that love, whose view is muffled still,

Should without eyes see pathways to his will!
Where shall we dine? O me! What fray was here?
Yet tell me not, for I have heard it all.
Here's much to do with hate, but more with love.
Why then, O brawling love! O loving hate!
O anything, of nothing first create!
O heavy lightness! serious vanity!
Mis-shapen chaos of well-seeming forms!
Feather of lead, bright smoke, cold fire, sick health!
Still-waking sleep, that is not what it is!
This love feel I, that feel no love in this.
Dost thou not laugh?

BENVOLIO: No, coz, I rather weep.

ROMEO: Good heart, at what?

BENVOLIO: At thy good heart's oppression.

ROMEO: Why, such is love's transgression.
Griefs of mine own lie heavy in my breast,
Which thou wilt propagate, to have it prest
With more of thine. This love that thou hast shown
Doth add more grief to too much of mine own.
Love is a smoke raised with the fume of sighs;
Being purged, a fire sparkling in lovers' eyes;
Being vex'd, a sea nourish'd with loving tears.
What is it else? A madness most discreet,
A choking gall, and a preserving sweet.
Farewell, my coz.

BENVOLIO: Soft! I will go along;
An if you leave me so, you do me wrong.

ROMEO: Tut, I have lost myself; I am not here:
This is not Romeo, he's some other where.

BENVOLIO: Tell me in sadness who is that you love.

ROMEO: What, shall I groan and tell thee?
BENVOLIO: Groan! why, no; But sadly tell me who.
ROMEO: Bid a sick man in sadness make his will.
    Ah, word ill urged to one that is so ill!
    In sadness, cousin, I do love a woman.
BENVOLIO: I aim'd so near, when I supposed you loved.
ROMEO: A right good mark man! And she's fair I love.
BENVOLIO: A right fair mark, fair coz, is soonest hit.
ROMEO: Well, in that hit you miss: she'll not be hit
    With Cupid's arrow. She hath Dian's wit,
    And in strong proof of chastity well arm'd,
    From Love's weak childish bow she lives unharm'd.
    She will not stay the siege of loving terms,
    Nor bide the encounter of assailing eyes,
    Nor ope her lap to saint-seducing gold.
    O, she is rich in beauty; only poor,
    That, when she dies, with beauty dies her store.
BENVOLIO: Then she hath sworn that she will still live chaste?
ROMEO: She hath, and in that sparing makes huge waste;
    For beauty, starved with her severity,
    Cuts beauty off from all posterity.
    She is too fair, too wise, wisely too fair,
    To merit bliss by making me despair.
    She hath forsworn to love, and in that vow
    Do I live dead that live to tell it now.
BENVOLIO: Be ruled by me: forget to think of her.
ROMEO: O, teach me how I should forget to think!
BENVOLIO: By giving liberty unto thine eyes.
    Examine other beauties.
ROMEO: 'Tis the way
    To call hers, exquisite, in question more.
    These happy masks that kiss fair ladies' brows,

Being black, puts us in mind they hide the fair.
He that is strucken blind cannot forget
The precious treasure of his eyesight lost.
Show me a mistress that is passing fair,
What doth her beauty serve, but as a note
Where I may read who pass'd that passing fair?
Farewell; thou canst not teach me to forget.

BENVOLIO: I'll pay that doctrine or else die in debt.

Exeunt

Scene II—*A street*

Enter CAPULET, COUNTY PARIS, and the CLOWN, his Servant

CAPULET: But Montague is bound as well as I,
In penalty alike; and 'tis not hard, I think,
For men so old as we to keep the peace.

PARIS: Of honourable reckoning are you both,
And pity 'tis you lived at odds so long.
But now, my lord, what say you to my suit?

CAPULET: But saying o'er what I have said before:
My child is yet a stranger in the world,
She hath not seen the change of fourteen years;
Let two more summers wither in their pride
Ere we may think her ripe to be a bride.

PARIS: Younger than she are happy mothers made.

CAPULET: And too soon marr'd are those so early made.
Earth hath swallow'd all my hopes but she;
She is the hopeful lady of my earth.
But woo her, gentle Paris, get her heart;
My will to her consent is but a part.

And, she agreed, within her scope of choice
Lies my consent and fair according voice.
This night I hold an old accustom'd feast,
Whereto I have invited many a guest,
Such as I love; and you among the store,
One more, most welcome, makes my number more.
At my poor house look to behold this night
Earth-treading stars that make dark heaven light.
Such comfort as do lusty young men feel
When well-apparell'd April on the heel
Of limping winter treads, even such delight
Among fresh female buds shall you this night
Inherit at my house. Hear all, all see,
And like her most whose merit most shall be;
Which on more view of many, mine, being one,
May stand in number, though in reckoning none.
Come, go with me.

To Servant, giving him a paper

Go, sirrah, trudge about
Through fair Verona; find those persons out
Whose names are written there, and to them say
My house and welcome on their pleasure stay.

Exeunt CAPULET and PARIS

SERVANT: Find them out whose names are written here! It is written that the shoemaker should meddle with his yard and the tailor with his last, the fisher with his pencil and the painter with his nets; but I am sent to find those persons whose names are here writ, and can never find what names the writing person hath here writ. I must to the learned. In good time!

Enter BENVOLIO and ROMEO

BENVOLIO: Tut, man, one fire burns out another's burning,

One pain is lessen'd by another's anguish;
Turn giddy, and be holp by backward turning;
One desperate grief cures with another's languish.
Take thou some new infection to thy eye,
And the rank poison of the old will die.

ROMEO: Your plaintain leaf is excellent for that.

BENVOLIO: For what, I pray thee?

ROMEO: For your broken shin.

BENVOLIO: Why, Romeo, art thou mad?

ROMEO: Not mad, but bound more than a mad-man is;
Shut up in prison, kept without my food,
Whipt and tormented, and—God-den, good fellow.

SERVANT: God gi' god'den. I pray, sir, can you read?

ROMEO: Ay, mine own fortune in my misery.

SERVANT: Perhaps you have learned it without book. But I pray, can you read anything you see?

ROMEO: Ay, if I know the letters and the language.

SERVANT: Ye say honestly; rest you merry!

ROMEO: Stay, fellow; I can read.

[*He reads the list*] 'Signior Martino and his wife and daughters; County Anselme and his beauteous sisters; the lady widow of Vitravio; Signior Placentio and his lovely nieces; Mercutio and his brother Valentine; mine uncle Capulet, his wife, and daughters; my fair niece Rosaline and Livia; Signior Valentio and his cousin Tybalt; Lucio and the lively Helena.' A fair assembly. [*Gives back the paper*] Whither should they come?

SERVANT: Up.

ROMEO: Whither?

SERVANT: To supper. To our house.

ROMEO: Whose house?

SERVANT: My master's.

ROMEO: Indeed, I should have ask'd you that before.

SERVANT: Now I'll tell you without asking: my master is the

great rich Capulet; and if you be not of the house of Montagues, I pray come and crush a cup of wine. Rest you merry!

Exit

BENVOLIO: At this same ancient feast of Capulet's
Sups the fair Rosaline whom thou so lovest
With all the admired beauties of Verona.
Go thither, and with unattainted eye
Compare her face with some that I shall show,
And I will make thee think thy swan a crow.
ROMEO: When the devout religion of mine eye
Maintains such falsehood, then turn tears to fires;
And these, who, often drown'd, could never die,
Transparent heretics, be burnt for liars!
One fairer than my love! The all-seeing sun
Ne'er saw her match since first the world begun.
BENVOLIO: Tut, you saw her fair, none else being by,
Herself poised with herself in either eye;
But in that crystal scales let there be weigh'd
Your lady's love against some other maid
That I will show you shining at this feast,
And she shall scant show well that now seems best.
ROMEO: I'll go along, no such sight to be shown,
But to rejoice in splendor of mine own.

Exeunt

SCENE III—*Capulet's house*

Enter LADY CAPULET and Nurse

LADY CAPULET: Nurse, where's my daughter? Call her forth to me.
NURSE: Now, by my maidenhead, at twelve year old,
I bade her come. What, lamb! what, ladybird!

God forbid! Where's this girl? What, Juliet!

Enter JULIET

JULIET: How now, who calls?
NURSE: Your mother.
JULIET: Madam, I am here. What is your will?
LADY CAPULET: This is the matter. Nurse, give leave awhile,
We must talk in secret. Nurse, come back again;
I have remember'd me, thou's hear our counsel.
Thou know'st my daughter's of a pretty age.
NURSE: Faith, I can tell her age unto an hour.
LADY CAPULET: She's not fourteen.
NURSE: I'll lay fourteen of my teeth—
And yet, to my teeth be it spoken, I have but four—
She is not fourteen. How long is it now
To Lammas-tide?
LADY CAPULET: A fortnight and odd days.
NURSE: Even or odd, of all days in the year,
Come Lammas Eve at night shall she be fourteen.
Susan and she—God rest all Christian souls!—
Were of an age. Well, Susan is with God;
She was too good for me. But, as I said,
On Lammas Eve at night shall she be fourteen;
That shall she, marry; I remember it well.
'Tis since the earthquake now eleven years;
And she was wean'd—I never shall forget it—
Of all the days of the year, upon that day;
For I had then laid wormwood to my dug,
Sitting in the sun under the dove-house wall;
My lord and you were then at Mantua.
Nay, I do bear a brain. But, as I said,
When it did taste the wormwood on the nipple
Of my dug, and felt it bitter, pretty fool,

To see it tetchy, and fall out with the dug!
Shake, quoth the dove-house. 'Twas no need, I trow,
To bid me trudge:
And since that time it is eleven years;
For then she could stand high-lone; nay, by the rood,
She could have run and waddled all about;
For even the day before, she broke her brow;
And then my husband—God be with his soul!
'A was a merry man—took up the child.
'Yea,' quoth he, 'dost thou fall upon thy face?
Thou wilt fall backward when thou hast more wit,
Wilt thou not, Jule?' And, by my holidam
The pretty wretch left crying, and said 'Ay'.
To see, now, how a jest shall come about!
I warrant, an I should live a thousand years,
I never should forget it: 'Wilt thou not, Jule?' quoth he;
And, pretty fool, it stinted and said 'Ay'.

LADY CAPULET: Enough of this; I pray thee hold thy peace.

NURSE: Yes, madam. Yet I cannot choose but laugh
To think it should leave crying and say 'Ay'.
And yet, I warrant, it had upon its brow
A bump as big as a young cockerel's stone—
A parlous knock; and it cried bitterly.
'Yea,' quoth my husband 'fall'st upon thy face?
Thou wilt fall backward when thou comest to age;
Wilt thou not, Jule?' It stinted, and said 'Ay'.

JULIET: And stint thou too, I pray thee, nurse, say I.

NURSE: Peace, I have done. God mark thee to his grace!
Thou wast the prettiest babe that e'er I nursed;
An I might live to see thee married once,
I have my wish.

LADY CAPULET: Marry, that 'marry' is the very theme

I came to talk of. Tell me, daughter Juliet,
How stands your disposition to be married?
JULIET: It is an honour that I dream not of.
NURSE: An honour! Were not I thine only nurse,
I would say thou hadst suck'd wisdom from thy teat.
LADY CAPULET: Well, think of marriage now. Younger than you,
Here in Verona, ladies of esteem,
Are made already mothers. By my count,
I was your mother much upon these years
That you are now a maid. Thus, then, in brief:
The valiant Paris seeks you for his love.
NURSE: A man, young lady! lady, such a man
As all the world—why, he's a man of wax.
LADY CAPULET: Verona's summer hath not such a flower.
NURSE: Nay, he's a flower; in faith, a very flower.
LADY CAPULET: What say you? Can you love the gentleman?
This night you shall behold him at our feast;
Read o'er the volume of young Paris' face,
And find delight writ there with beauty's pen;
Examine every married lineament,
And see how one another lends content;
And what obscured in this fair volume lies
Find written in the margent of his eyes.
This precious book of love, this unbound lover,
To beautify him, only lacks a cover.
The fish lives in the sea, and 'tis much pride
For fair without the fair within to hide.
That book in many's eyes doth share the glory
That in gold clasps locks in the golden story;
So shall you share all that he doth possess,
By having him making yourself no less.

NURSE: No less! Nay, bigger; women grow by men.
LADY CAPULET: Speak briefly, can you like of Paris' love?
JULIET: I'll look to like, if looking liking move;
  But no more deep will I endart mine eye
  Than your consent gives strength to make it fly.

Enter a Servant

SERVANT: Madam, the guests are come, supper served up, you called, my young lady asked for, the nurse cursed in the pantry, and everything in extremity. I must hence to wait; I beseech you, follow straight.

LADY CAPULET: We follow thee.

Exit Servant

  Juliet, the County stays.
NURSE: Go, girl, seek happy nights to happy days.

Exeunt

Scene IV—A *street*

Enter ROMEO, MERCUTIO, BENVOLIO, with five or six other Maskers; Torch-bearers

ROMEO: What, shall this speech be spoke for our excuse?
  Or shall we on without apology?
BENVOLIO: The date is out of such prolixity.
  We'll have no Cupid hoodwink'd with a scarf,
  Bearing a Tartar's painted bow of lath,
  Scaring the ladies like a crow-keeper;
  Nor no without-book prologue, faintly spoke
  After the prompter, for our entrance;
  But, let them measure us by what they will,
  We'll measure them a measure, and be gone.
ROMEO: Give me a torch; I am not for this ambling;

Being but heavy, I will bear the light.
MERCUTIO: Nay, gentle Romeo, we must have you dance.
ROMEO: Not I, believe me. You have dancing shoes
With nimble soles: I have a soul of lead
So stakes me to the ground I cannot move.
MERCUTIO: You are a lover; borrow Cupid's wings
And soar with them above a common bound.
ROMEO: I am too sore enpierced with his shaft
To soar with his light feathers; and so bound
I cannot bound a pitch above dull woe.
Under love's heavy burden do I sink.
MERCUTIO: And to sink in it should you burden love;
Too great oppression for a tender thing.
ROMEO: Is love a tender thing? It is too rough,
Too rude, too boisterous, and it pricks like thorn.
MERCUTIO: If love be rough with you, be rough with love;
Prick love for pricking, and you beat love down.
Give me a case to put my visage in.

Putting on a mask

A visor for a visor! What care I
What curious eye doth quote deformities?
Here are the beetle brows shall blush for me.
BENVOLIO: Come, knock and enter; and no sooner in
But every man betake him to his legs.
ROMEO: A torch for me. Let wantons, light of heart,
Tickle the senseless rushes with their heels;
For I am proverb'd with a grandsire phrase;
I'll be a candle-holder and look on;
The game was ne'er so fair, and I am done.
MERCUTIO: Tut, dun's the mouse, the constable's own word;
If thou art Dun, we'll draw thee from the mire
Of this sir-reverence love, wherein thou stick'st

Up to the ears. Come, we burn daylight, ho!
ROMEO: Nay, that's not so.
MERCUTIO: I mean, sir, in delay
We waste our lights in vain—like lamps by day.
Take our good meaning, for our judgment sits
Five times in that ere once in our five wits.
ROMEO: And we mean well in going to this mask;
But 'tis no wit to go.
MERCUTIO: Why, may one ask?
ROMEO: I dreamt a dream to-night.
MERCUTIO: And so did I.
ROMEO: Well, what was yours?
MERCUTIO: That dreamers often lie.
ROMEO: In bed asleep, while they do dream things true.
MERCUTIO: O, then I see Queen Mab hath been with you.
She is the fairies' midwife, and she comes
In shape no bigger than an agate stone
On the fore-finger of an alderman,
Drawn with a team of little atomies
Athwart men's noses as they lie asleep;
Her waggon-spokes made of long spiders' legs;
The cover, of the wings of grasshoppers;
Her traces, of the smallest spider's web;
Her collars, of the moonshine's watery beams;
Her whip, of cricket's bone; the lash, of film,
Her waggoner, a small grey-coated gnat,
Not half so big as a round little worm
Prick'd from the lazy finger of a maid.
Her chariot is an empty hazel-nut,
Made by the joiner squirrel or old grub,
Time out o' mind the fairies' coachmakers.
And in this state she gallops night by night

Through lovers' brains, and then they dream of love;
O'er courtiers' knees, that dream on court'sies straight;
O'er lawyers' fingers, who straight dream on fees;
O'er ladies 'lips, who straight on kisses dream,
Which oft the angry Mab with blisters plagues,
Because their breaths with sweetmeats tainted are.
Sometime she gallops o'er a courtier's nose,
And then dreams he of smelling out a suit;
And sometime comes she with a tithe-pig's tail,
Tickling a parson's nose as 'a lies asleep
Then dreams he of another benefice.
Sometime she driveth o'er a soldier's neck,
And then dreams he of cutting foreign throats,
Of breaches, ambuscadoes, Spanish blades,
Of healths five-fathom deep; and then anon
Drums in his ear, at which he starts and wakes,
And, being thus frighted, swears a prayer or two,
And sleeps again. This is that very Mab
That plats the manes of horses in the night;
And bakes the elflocks in foul sluttish hairs,
Which once untangled, much misfortune bodes.
This is the hag, when maids lie on their backs,
That presses them and learns them first to bear,
Making them women of good carriage.
This is she—

ROMEO: Peace, peace, Mercutio, peace!
Thou talk'st of nothing.

MERCUTIO: True, I talk of dreams,
Which are the children of an idle brain,
Begot of nothing but vain fantasy;
Which is as thin of substance as the air,
And more inconstant than the wind, who woos

Even now the frozen bosom of the north,
And, being anger'd, puffs away from thence,
Turning his side to the dew-dropping south.

BENVOLIO: This wind you talk of blows us from ourselves:
Supper is done, and we shall come too late.

ROMEO: I fear, too early; for my mind misgives
Some consequence, yet hanging in the stars,
Shall bitterly begin his fearful date
With this night's revels and expire the term
Of a despised life closed in my breast,
By some vile forfeit of untimely death.
But He that hath the steerage of my course
Direct my sail! On, lusty gentlemen.

BENVOLIO: Strike, drum.

They march about the stage

Exeunt

Scene V—*Capulet's house*

Enter the Maskers. Servingmen come forth with napkins

FIRST SERVANT: Where's Potpan, that he helps not to take away? He shift a trencher? He scrape a trencher!

SECOND SERVANT: When good manners shall lie all in one or two men's hands, and they unwashed too, 'tis a foul thing.

FIRST SERVANT: Away with the join-stools, remove the court-cubbert, look to the plate. Good thou, save me a piece of marchpane; and as thou lovest me let the porter let in Susan Grindstone and Nell. Antony, and Potpan!

SECOND SERVANT: Ay, boy, ready.

FIRST SERVANT: You are looked for and called for, asked for and sought for, in the great chamber.

THIRD SERVANT: We cannot be here and there too. Cheerly, boys! Be brisk a while, and the longer liver take all!

Servants retire

Enter CAPULET, with all the Guests and Gentlewomen to the Maskers

CAPULET: Welcome, gentlemen! Ladies that have their toes
Unplagued with corns will have a bout with you.
Ah ha, my mistresses! which of you all
Will now deny to dance? She that makes dainty,
She I'll swear hath corns; am I come near ye now?
Welcome, gentlemen! I have seen the day
That I have worn a visor and could tell
A whispering tale in a fair lady's ear,
Such as would please: 'Tis gone, 'tis gone, 'tis gone!
You are welcome, gentlemen. Come, musicians, play.
A hall, a hall! give room; and foot it, girls.

Music plays, and they dance

More light, you knaves; and turn the tables up,
And quench the fire, the room is grown too hot.
Ah, sirrah, this unlook'd-for sport comes well.
Nay, sit, nay, sit, good cousin Capulet,
For you and I are past our dancing days.
How long is't now since last yourself and I
Were in a mask?

SECOND CAPULET: By'r Lady, thirty years.

CAPULET: What, man! 'tis not so much, 'tis not so much.
'Tis since the nuptials of Lucentio,
Come Pentecost as quickly as it will,
Some five and twenty years; and then we mask'd.

SECOND CAPULET: 'Tis more, 'tis more: his son is elder, sir;
His son is thirty.

CAPULET: Will you tell me that?
His son was but a ward two years ago.
ROMEO: [*To a Servant*] What lady is that which doth enrich the hand
Of yonder knight?
SERVANT: I know not, sir.
ROMEO: O, she doth teach the torches to burn bright!
It seems she hangs upon the cheek of night
As a rich jewel in an Ethiope's ear—
Beauty too rich for use, for earth too dear!
So shows a snowy dove trooping with crows
As yonder lady o'er her fellows shows.
The measure done, I'll watch her place of stand,
And, touching hers, make blessed my rude hand.
Did my heart love till now? Forswear it, sight;
For I ne'er saw true beauty till this night.
TYBALT: This, by his voice, should be a Montague.
Fetch me my rapier, boy. What, dares the slave
Come hither, cover'd with an antic face,
To fleer and scorn at our solemnity?
Now, by the stock and honour of my kin,
To strike him dead I hold it not a sin.
CAPULET: Why, how now, kinsman! Wherefore storm you so?
TYBALT: Uncle, this is a Montague, our foe;
A villain, that is hither come in spite
To scorn at our solemnity this night.
CAPULET: Young Romeo, is it?
TYBALT: 'Tis he, that villain Romeo.
CAPULET: Content thee, gentle coz, let him alone.
'A bears him like a portly gentleman;
And, to say truth, Verona brags of him
To be a virtuous and well-govern'd youth.
I would not for the wealth of all this town

Here in my house do him disparagement.
Therefore be patient, take no note of him;
It is my will; the which if thou respect,
Show a fair presence and put off these frowns,
An ill-beseeming semblance for a feast.

TYBALT: It fits, when such a villain is a guest.
I'll not endure him.

CAPULET: He shall be endured.
What, goodman boy! I say, he shall. Go to;
Am I the master here or you? Go to.
You'll not endure him! God shall mend my soul!
You'll make a mutiny among my guests!
You will set cock-a-hoop! You'll be the man!

TYBALT: Why, uncle, 'tis a shame.

CAPULET: Go to, go to;
You are a saucy boy. Is't so, indeed?
This trick may chance to scathe you. I know what:
You must contrary me! Marry, 'tis time.
Well said, my hearts!—You are a princox; go.
Be quiet, or—More light, more light!—For shame!
I'll make you quiet. What!—Cheerly, my hearts!

TYBALT: Patience perforce with wilful choler meeting
Makes my flesh tremble in their different greeting.
I will withdraw; but this intrusion shall,
Now seeming sweet, convert to bitterest gall.

Exit

ROMEO: [*To JULIET*] If I profane with my unworthiest hand
This holy shrine, the gentle fine is this:
My lips, two blushing pilgrims, ready stand
To smooth that rough touch with a tender kiss.

JULIET: Good pilgrim, you do wrong your hand too much,

Which mannerly devotion shows in this;
For saints have hands that pilgrims' hands do touch,
And palm to palm is holy palmers' kiss.
ROMEO: Have not saints lips, and holy palmers too?
JULIET: Ay, pilgrim, lips that they must use in prayer.
ROMEO: O, then, dear saint, let lips do what hands do!
They pray; grant thou, lest faith turn to despair.
JULIET: Saints do not move, though grant for prayers' sake.
ROMEO: Then move not while my prayer's effect I take.
Thus from my lips by thine, my sin is purged.
JULIET: Then have my lips the sin that they have took.
ROMEO: Sin from thy lips? O trespass sweetly urged!
Give me my sin again.

Kissing her

JULIET: You kiss by the book.
NURSE: Madam, your mother craves a word with you.
ROMEO: What is her mother?
NURSE: Marry, bachelor,
Her mother is the lady of the house,
And a good lady, and a wise and virtuous.
I nursed her daughter that you talk'd withal.
I tell you, he that can lay hold of her
Shall have the chinks.
ROMEO: Is she a Capulet?
O dear account! my life is my foe's debt.
BENVOLIO: Away, be gone; the sport is at the best.
ROMEO: Ay, so I fear; the more is my unrest.
CAPULET: Nay, gentlemen, prepare not to be gone;
We have a trifling foolish banquet towards.
Is it e'en so? Why, then I thank you all;
I thank you, honest gentlemen; good night.

More torches here! [*Exeunt Maskers*] Come on then, let's to bed.

Ah, sirrah, by my fay, it waxes late;
I'll to my rest.

Exeunt all but JULIET and NURSE

JULIET: Come hither, nurse. What is yond gentleman?
NURSE: The son and heir of old Tiberio.
JULIET: What's he that now is going out of door?
NURSE: Marry, that I think be young Petrucio.
JULIET: What's he that follows there, that would not dance?
NURSE: I know not.
JULIET: Go ask his name.—if he be married,
My grave is like to be my wedding bed.
NURSE: His name is Romeo, and a Montague;
The only son of your great enemy.
JULIET: My only love sprung from my only hate!
Too early seen unknown, and known too late!
Prodigious birth of love it is to me,
That I must love a loathed enemy.
NURSE: What's this? what's this?
JULIET: A rhyme I learnt even now
Of one I danced withal.

One calls within 'Juliet'.

NURSE: Anon, anon!
Come, let's away; the strangers all are gone.

Exeunt

Act II

Prologue

Enter CHORUS

Now old desire doth in his death-bed lie,
And young affection gapes to be his heir;
That fair for which love groan'd for and would die,
With tender Juliet match'd, is now not fair.
Now Romeo is beloved and loves again,
Alike betwitched by the charm of looks;
But to his foe supposed he must complain,
And she steal love's sweet bait from fearful hooks.
Being held a foe, he may not have access
To breathe such vows as lovers use to swear;
And she as much in love, her means much less
To meet her new beloved any where.
But passion lends them power, time means, to meet;
Tempering extremities with extreme sweet.

Exit

Scene I—*A lane by the wall of Capulet's orchard*

Enter ROMEO

ROMEO: Can I go forward when my heart is here?
Turn back, dull earth, and find thy centre out.

He climbs the wall and leaps down within it

Enter BENVOLIO and MERCUTIO

BENVOLIO: Romeo! my cousin, Romeo!
MERCUTIO: He is wise,
And, on my life, hath stol'n him home to bed.
BENVOLIO: He ran this way, and leapt this orchard wall.
Call, good Mercutio.
MERCUTIO: Nay, I'll conjure too.
Romeo! humours! madman! passion! lover!
Appear thou in the likeness of a sigh;
Speak but one rhyme and I am satisfied;
Cry but 'Ay me!' pronounce but 'love' and 'dove';
Speak to my gossip Venus one fair word,
One nick name for her purblind son and heir,
Young Adam Cupid, he that shot so trim
When King Cophetua loved the beggar-maid!
He heareth not, he stirreth not, he moveth not;
The ape is dead, and I must conjure him.
I conjure thee by Rosaline's bright eyes,
By her high forehead and her scarlet lip,
By her fine foot, straight leg, and quivering thigh,
And the demesnes that there adjacent lie,
That in thy likeness thou appear to us.
BENVOLIO: And if he hear thee, thou wilt anger him.
MERCUTIO: This cannot anger him: 'twould anger him
To raise a spirit in his mistress' circle
Of some strange nature, letting it there stand
Till she had laid it and conjured it down;
That were some spite. My invocation
Is fair and honest: in his mistress' name,
I conjure only but to raise up him.
BENVOLIO: Come, he hath hid himself among these trees
To be consorted with the humorous night:
Blind is his love, and best befits the dark.

MERCUTIO: If love be blind, love cannot hit the mark.
Now will he sit under a medlar tree,
And wish his mistress were that kind of fruit
As maids call medlars when they laugh alone.
O Romeo, that she were, O that she were
An open et cetera, thou a poperin pear!
Romeo, good night. I'll to my truckle bed;
This field-bed is too cold for me to sleep.
Come, shall we go?
BENVOLIO: Go, then; for 'tis in vain
To seek him here that means not to be found.

Exeunt

Scene II—*Capulet's orchard*

Enter ROMEO

ROMEO: He jests at scars that never felt a wound.

Enter JULIET above at a window

But, soft! What light through yonder window breaks?
It is the east, and Juliet is the sun.
Arise, fair sun, and kill the envious moon,
Who is already sick and pale with grief
That thou her maid art far more fair than she.
Be not her maid, since she is envious;
Her vestal livery is but sick and green,
And none but fools do wear it; cast it off.
It is my lady; O, it is my love!
O that she knew she were!
She speaks, yet she says nothing. What of that?
Her eye discourses; I will answer it.
I am too bold, 'tis not to me she speaks;

Two of the fairest stars in all the heaven,
Having some business, do entreat her eyes
To twinkle in their spheres till they return.
What if her eyes were there, they in her head?
The brightness of her cheek would shame those stars,
As daylight doth a lamp; her eyes in heaven
Would through the airy region stream so bright
That birds would sing, and think it were not night.
See how she leans her cheek upon her hand!
O that I were a glove upon that hand,
That I might touch that cheek!

JULIET: Ay me!

ROMEO: She speaks.
O, speak again, bright angel, for thou art
As glorious to this night, being o'er my head,
As is a winged messenger of heaven
Unto the white-upturned wondering eyes
Of mortals that fall back to gaze on him,
When he bestrides the lazy-pacing clouds
And sails upon the bosom of the air.

JULIET: O Romeo, Romeo! wherefore art thou Romeo?
Deny thy father and refuse thy name;
Or, if thou wilt not, be but sworn my love,
And I'll no longer be a Capulet.

ROMEO: [*Aside*] Shall I hear more, or shall I speak at this?

JULIET: 'Tis but thy name that is my enemy;
Thou art thyself, though not a Montague.
What's Montague? It is nor hand, nor foot,
Nor arm, nor face, nor any other part
Belonging to a man. O, be some other name!
What's in a name? That which we call a rose
By any other name would smell as sweet;

So Romeo would, were he not Romeo call'd,
Retain that dear perfection which he owes
Without that title. Romeo, doff thy name;
And for thy name, which is no part of thee,
Take all myself.

ROMEO: I take thee at thy word:
Call me but love, and I'll be new baptized;
Henceforth I never will be Romeo.

JULIET: What man art thou, that, thus bescreen'd in night,
So stumblest on my counsel?

ROMEO: By a name
I know not how to tell thee who I am:
My name, dear saint, is hateful to myself,
Because it is an enemy to thee;
Had I it written, I would tear the word.

JULIET: My ears have not yet drunk a hundred words
Of thy tongue's uttering, yet I know the sound:
Art thou not Romeo, and a Montague?

ROMEO: Neither, fair maid, if either thee dislike.

JULIET: How camest thou hither, tell me, and wherefore?
The orchard walls are high and hard to climb;
And the place death, considering who thou art,
If any of my kinsmen find thee here.

ROMEO: With love's light wings did I o'er-perch these walls,
For stony limits cannot hold love out;
And what love can do, that dares love attempt.
Therefore thy kinsmen are no let to me.

JULIET: If they do see thee, they will murder thee.

ROMEO: Alack, there lies more peril in thine eye
Than twenty of their swords; look thou but sweet,
And I am proof against their enmity.

JULIET: I would not for the world they saw thee here.

ROMEO: I have night's cloak to hide me from their eyes;
And but thou love me, let them find me here.
My life were better ended by their hate
Than death prorogued wanting of thy love.
JULIET: By whose direction found'st thou out this place?
ROMEO: By love, that first did prompt me to enquire;
He lent me counsel, and I lent him eyes.
I am no pilot; yet, wert thou as far
As that vast shore wash'd with the farthest sea,
I should adventure for such merchandise.
JULIET: Thou know'st the mask of night is on my face,
Else would a maiden blush bepaint my cheek
For that which thou hast heard me speak to-night.
Fain would I dwell on form, fain, fain deny
What I have spoke; but farewell compliment!
Dost thou love me? I know thou wilt say ay,
And I will take thy word; yet, if thou swear'st,
Thou mayst prove false; at lovers' perjuries
They say Jove laughs. O gentle Romeo,
If thou dost love, pronounce it faithfully.
Or, if thou think'st I am too quickly won,
I'll frown, and be perverse, an say thee nay,
So thou wilt woo; but else, not for the world.
In truth, fair Montague, I am too fond;
And therefore thou mayst think my havior light;
But trust me, gentleman, I'll prove more true
Than those that have more cunning to be strange.
I should have been more strange, I must confess,
But that thou overheard'st, ere I was ware,
My true love's passion. Therefore pardon me,
And not impute this yielding to light love,
Which the dark night hath so discovered.

ROMEO: Lady, by yonder blessed moon I vow,
That tips with silver all these fruit-tree tops—
JULIET: O, swear not by the moon, the inconstant moon,
That monthly changes in her circled orb,
Lest that thy love prove likewise variable.
ROMEO: What shall I swear by?
JULIET: Do not swear at all;
Or, if thou wilt, swear by thy gracious self,
Which is the god of my idolatry,
And I'll believe thee.
ROMEO: If my heart's dear love—
JULIET: Well, do not swear. Although I joy in thee,
I have no joy of this contract to-night:
It is too rash, too unadvised, too sudden;
Too like the lightning, which doth cease to be
Ere one can say 'It lightens'. Sweet, good night!
This bud of love, by summer's ripening breath,
May prove a beauteous flower when next we meet.
Good night, good night! As sweet repose and rest
Come to thy heart as that within my breast!
ROMEO: O, wilt thou leave me so unsatisfied?
JULIET: What satisfaction canst thou have to-night?
ROMEO: The exchange of thy love's faithful vow for mine.
JULIET: I gave thee mine before thou didst request it;
And yet I would it were to give again.
ROMEO: Wouldst thou withdraw it? For what purpose, love?
JULIET: But to be frank, and give it thee again.
And yet I wish but for the thing I have.
My bounty is as boundless as the sea,
My love as deep: the more I give to thee,
The more I have, for both are infinite.

Nurse calls within

I hear some noise within. Dear love, adieu!—
Anon, good nurse!—Sweet Montague, be true.
Stay but a little, I will come again.

Exit

ROMEO: O blessed, blessed night! I am afeard.
Being in night, all this is but a dream,
Too flattering-sweet to be substantial.

Re-enter JULIET above

JULIET: Three words, dear Romeo, and good night indeed.
If that thy bent of love be honourable,
Thy purpose marriage, send me word to-morrow,
By one that I'll procure to come to thee,
Where and what time thou wilt perform the rite;
And all my fortunes at thy foot I'll lay,
And follow thee, my lord, throughout the world.
NURSE: [*Within*] Madam!
JULIET: I come, anon.—But if thou mean'st not well,
I do beseech thee—
NURSE: [*Within*] Madam!
JULIET: By and by, I come—
To cease thy suit, and leave me to my grief.
To-morrow will I send.
ROMEO: So thrive my soul—
JULIET: A thousand times good night!

Exit

ROMEO: A thousand times the worse, to want thy light.
Love goes toward love as school-boys from their books;
But love from love, toward school with heavy looks.

Re-enter JULIET above

JULIET: Hist! Romeo, hist!—O for a falc'ner's voice,

To lure this tassel-gentle back again!
Bondage is hoarse, and may not speak aloud;
Else would I tear the cave where Echo lies,
And make her airy tongue more hoarse than mine
With repetition of my Romeo's name.
Romeo!

ROMEO: It is my soul that calls upon my name.
How silver-sweet sound lovers' tongues by night,
Like softest music to attending ears!

JULIET: Romeo!

ROMEO: My dear?

JULIET: At what o'clock to-morrow
Shall I send to thee?

ROMEO: By the hour of nine.

JULIET: I will not fail. 'Tis twenty years till then.
I have forgot why I did call thee back.

ROMEO: Let me stand here till thou remember it.

JULIET: I shall forget, to have thee still stand there,
Remembering how I love thy company.

ROMEO: And I'll still stay, to have thee still forget,
Forgetting any other home but this.

JULIET: 'Tis almost morning. I would have thee gone:
And yet no further than a wanton's bird,
That lets it hop a little from her hand,
Like a poor prisoner in his twisted gyves,
And with a silk thread plucks it back again,
So loving-jealous of his liberty.

ROMEO: I would I were thy bird.

JULIET: Sweet, so would I.
Yet I should kill thee with much cherishing.
Good night, good night! Parting is such sweet sorrow
That I shall say good night till it be morrow.

Exit

ROMEO: Sleep dwell upon thine eyes, peace in thy breast!
Would I were sleep and peace, so sweet to rest!
Hence will I to my ghostly father's cell,
His help to crave and my dear hap to tell.

Exit

Scene III—*Friar Lawrence's cell*

Enter FRIAR LAWRENCE with a basket

FRIAR LAWRENCE: The grey-eyed morn smiles on the frowning night,
Checkering the eastern clouds with streaks of light;
And fleckel'd darkness like a drunkard reels
From forth day's path and Titan's fiery wheels.
Now, ere the sun advance his burning eye
The day to cheer and night's dank dew to dry,
I must up-fill this osier cage of ours
With baleful weeds and precious-juiced flowers.
The earth that's nature's mother is her tomb;
What is her burying grave, that is her womb.
And from her womb children of divers kind
We sucking on her natural bosom find;
Many for many virtues excellent,
None but for some, and yet all different.
O, mickle is the powerful grace that lies
In plants, herbs, stones, and their true qualities;
For nought so vile that on the earth doth live
But to the earth some special good doth give;
Nor aught so good but, strain'd from that fair use,
Revolts from true birth, stumbling on abuse:
Virtue itself turns vice, being misapplied,

And vice sometimes by action dignified.
Within the infant rind of this weak flower
Poison hath residence, and medicine power;
For this, being smelt, with that part cheers each part;
Being tasted, slays all senses with the heart.
Two such opposed kings encamp them still
In man as well as herbs—grace and rude will;
And where the worser is predominant,
Full soon the canker death eats up that plant.

Enter ROMEO

ROMEO: Good morrow, father!

FRIAR LAWRENCE: Benedicite!
What early tongue so sweet saluteth me?
Young son, it argues a distemper'd head
So soon to bid good morrow to thy bed.
Care keeps his watch in every old man's eye,
And where care lodges sleep will never lie;
But where unbruised youth with unstuff'd brain
Doth couch his limbs, there golden sleep doth reign.
Therefore thy earliness doth me assure
Thou art uproused by some distemperature;
Or if not so, then here I hit it right—
Our Romeo hath not been in bed to-night.

ROMEO: That last is true; the sweeter rest was mine.

FRIAR LAWRENCE: God pardon sin! Wast thou with Rosaline?

ROMEO: With Rosaline, my ghostly father? No;
I have forgot that name, and that name's woe.

FRIAR LAWRENCE: That's my good son; but where hast thou been then?

ROMEO: I'll tell thee ere thou ask it me again.
I have been feasting with mine enemy;

Where, on a sudden, one hath wounded me
That's by me wounded; both our remedies
Within thy help and holy physic lies.
I bear no hatred, blessed man, for, lo,
My intercession likewise steads my foe.

FRIAR LAWRENCE: Be plain, good son, and homely in thy drift;
Riddling confession finds but riddling shrift.

ROMEO: Then plainly know my heart's dear love is set
On the fair daughter of rich Capulet.
As mine on hers, so hers is set on mine;
And all combined, save what thou must combine
By holy marriage. When, and where, and how,
We met, we woo'd, and made exchange of vow,
I'll tell thee as we pass; but this I pray,
That thou consent to marry us to-day.

FRIAR LAWRENCE: Holy Saint Francis! What a change is here!
Is Rosaline, that thou didst love so dear,
So soon forsaken? Young men's love, then, lies
Not truly in their hearts, but in their eyes.
Jesu Maria, what a deal of brine
Hath wash'd thy sallow cheeks for Rosaline!
How much salt water thrown away in waste,
To season love, that of it doth not taste!
The sun not yet thy sighs from heaven clears,
Thy old groans ring yet in my ancient ears;
Lo, here upon thy cheek the stain doth sit
Of an old tear that is not wash'd off yet.
If e'er thou wast thyself, and these woes thine,
Thou and these woes were all for Rosaline.
And art thou changed? Pronounce this sentence, then:
Women may fall, when there's no strength in men.

ROMEO: Thou chid'st me oft for loving Rosaline.
FRIAR LAWRENCE: For doting, not for loving, pupil mine.
ROMEO: And bad'st me bury love.
FRIAR LAWRENCE: Not in a grave
To lay one in, another out to have.
ROMEO: I pray thee chide not; her I love now
Doth grace for grace and love for love allow;
The other did not so.
FRIAR LAWRENCE: O, she knew well
Thy love did read by rote and could not spell.
But come, young waverer, come, go with me,
In one respect I'll thy assistant be;
For this alliance may so happy prove
To turn your households' rancour to pure love.
ROMEO: O, let us hence; I stand on sudden haste.
FRIAR LAWRENCE: Wisely and slow; they stumble that run fast.

Exeunt

SCENE IV—*A street*

Enter BENVOLIO and MERCUTIO

MERCUTIO: Where the devil should this Romeo be?
Came he not home to-night?
BENVOLIO: Not to his father's; I spoke with his man.
MERCUTIO: Why, that same pale hard-hearted wench, that Rosaline,
Torments him so that he will sure run mad.
BENVOLIO: Tybalt, the kinsman to old Capulet,
Hath sent a letter to his father's house.
MERCUTIO: A challenge, on my life.
BENVOLIO: Romeo will answer it.
MERCUTIO: Any man that can write may answer a letter.

BENVOLIO: Nay, he will answer the letter's master, how he dares, being dared.

MERCUTIO: Alas, poor Romeo, he is already dead: stabbed with a white wench's black eye; run through the ear with a love-song; the very pin of his heart cleft with the blind bow-boy's butt-shaft. And is he a man to encounter Tybalt?

BENVOLIO: Why, what is Tybalt?

MERCUTIO: More than Prince of Cats. O, he is the courageous captain of compliments. He fights as you sing prick-song: keeps time, distance, and proportion; he rests his minim rests, one, two, and the third in your bosom; the very butcher of a silk button, a duellist, a duellist; a gentleman of the very first house, of the first and second cause. Ah, the immortal passado! the punto reverso! The hai!—

BENVOLIO: The what?

MERCUTIO: The pox of such antic, lisping, affecting fantasticoes; these new tuners of accents!—'By Jesu, a very good blade! a very tall man! a very good whore!' Why, is not this a lamentable thing, grandsire, that we should be thus afflicted with these strange flies, these fashion-mongers, these pardon me's, who stand so much on the new form that they cannot at ease on the old bench? O, their bones, their bones!

Enter ROMEO

BENVOLIO: Here comes Romeo, here comes Romeo.

MERCUTIO: Without his roe, like a dried herring. flesh, flesh, how art thou fishified! Now is he for the numbers that Petrarch flowed in; Laura, to his lady, was a kitchen-wench; marry, she had a better love to be rhyme her; Dido, a dowdy; Cleopatra, a gipsy; Helen and Hero, hildings and harlots; Thisbe, a grey eye or so, but not to the purpose—Signior Romeo, bon jour! There's a French salutation to your French slop. You gave us the counterfeit fairly last night.

ROMEO: Good morrow to you both. What counterfeit did I give you?

MERCUTIO: The slip, sir, the slip; can you not conceive?

ROMEO: Pardon, good Mercutio, my business was great; and in such a case as mine a man may strain courtesy.

MERCUTIO: That's as much as to say, such a case as yours constrains a man to bow in the hams.

ROMEO: Meaning, to courtsy.

MERCUTIO: Thou hast most kindly hit it.

ROMEO: A most courteous exposition.

MERCUTIO: Nay, I am the very pink of courtesy.

ROMEO: Pink for flower.

MERCUTIO: Right.

ROMEO: Why, then is my pump well flowered.

MERCUTIO: Sure wit! Follow me this jest now till thou hast worn out thy pump, that, when the single sole of it is worn, the jest may remain, after the wearing, sole singular.

ROMEO: O single-soled jest, solely singular for the singleness!

MERCUTIO: Come between us, good Benvolio; my wits faints.

ROMEO: Swits and spurs, swits and spurs; or I'll cry a match.

MERCUTIO: Nay, if our wits run the wild-goose chase, I have done; for thou hast more of the wild; goose in one of thy wits than, I am sure, I have in my whole five. Was I with you there for the goose?

ROMEO: Thou wast never with me for anything when thou wast not there for the goose.

MERCUTIO: I will bite thee by the ear for that jest.

ROMEO: Nay, good goose, bite not.

MERCUTIO: Thy wit is a very bitter sweeting; it is a most sharp sauce.

ROMEO: And is it not then well served in to a sweet goose?

MERCUTIO: O, here's a wit of cheveril, that stretches from an inch narrow to an ell broad!

ROMEO: I stretch it out for that word 'broad', which, added to the goose, proves thee far and wide a broad goose.

MERCUTIO: Why, is not this better now than groaning for love? Now art thou sociable, now art thou Romeo; now art thou what thou art, by art as well as by nature; for this drivelling love is like a great natural that runs lolling up and down to hide his bauble in a hole.

BENVOLIO: Stop there, stop there.

MERCUTIO: Thou desirest me to stop in my tale against the hair.

BENVOLIO: Thou wouldst else have made thy tale large.

MERCUTIO: O, thou art deceived: I would have made it short; for I was come to the whole depth of my tale, and meant, indeed, to occupy the argument no longer.

ROMEO: Here's goodly gear!

Enter Nurse and her man, PETER

MERCUTIO: A sail, a sail!

BENVOLIO: Two, two; a shirt and a smock.

NURSE: Peter!

PETER: Anon.

NURSE: My fan, Peter.

MERCUTIO: Good Peter, to hide her face; for her fan's the fairer face.

NURSE: God ye good morrow, gentlemen.

MERCUTIO: God ye good den, fair gentlewoman.

NURSE: Is it good den?

MERCUTIO: 'Tis no less, I tell ye; for the bawdy hand of the dial is now upon the prick of noon.

NURSE: Out upon you! What a man are you?

ROMEO: One, gentlewoman, that God hath made himself to mar.

NURSE: By my troth, it is well said. 'For himself to mar' quoth 'a! Gentlemen, can any of you tell me where I may find the young Romeo?

ROMEO: I can tell you; but young Romeo will be older when you have found him than he was when you sought him. I am the youngest of that name, for fault of a worse.

NURSE: You say well.

MERCUTIO: Yea, is the worst well? Very well took, i' faith; wisely, wisely.

NURSE: if you be he, sir, I desire some confidence with you.

BENVOLIO: She will indite him to some supper.

MERCUTIO: A bawd, a bawd, a bawd! So ho!

ROMEO: What hast thou found?

MERCUTIO: No hare, sir; unless a hare, sir, in a lenten pie, that is something stale and hoar ere it be spent.

He walks by them and sings

An old hare hoar,
And an old hare hoar,
Is very good meat in Lent;
But a hare that is hoar
Is too much for a score,
When it hoars ere it be spent.

Romeo, will you come to your father's? We'll to dinner thither.

ROMEO: I will follow you.

MERCUTIO: Farewell, ancient lady; farewell,

Sings

lady, lady, lady.

Exeunt MERCUTIO and BENVOLIO

NURSE: I pray you, sir, what saucy merchant was this that was so full of his ropery?

ROMEO: A gentleman, nurse, that loves to hear himself talk, and will speak more in a minute than he will stand to in a month.

NURSE: An 'a speak anything against me, I'll take him down, an 'a were lustier than he is, and twenty such Jacks; and if I cannot, I'll find those that shall. Scurvy knave! I am none of his flirt-gills; I am none of his skains-mates. And thou must stand by too, and suffer every knave to use me at his pleasure?

PETER: I saw no man use you at his pleasure; if I had, my weapon should quickly have been out, I warrant you. I dare draw as soon as another man, if I see occasion in a good quarrel, and the law on my side.

NURSE: Now, afore God, I am so vexed that every part about me quivers. Scurvy knave!—Pray you, sir, a word; and as I told you, my young lady bid me enquire you out; what she bid me say I will keep to myself. But first let me tell ye, if ye should lead her in a fool's paradise, as they say, it were a very gross kind of behavior, as they say; for the gentlewoman is young; and, therefore, if you should deal double with her, truly it were an ill thing to be offered to any gentlewoman, and very weak dealing.

ROMEO: Nurse, commend me to thy lady and mistress. I protest unto thee—

NURSE: Good heart, and, i' faith, I will tell her as much. Lord, Lord! she will be a joyful woman.

ROMEO: What wilt thou tell her, nurse? Thou dost not mark me.

NURSE: I will tell her, sir, that you do protest; which, as I take it, is a gentleman-like offer.

ROMEO: Bid her devise

Some means to come to shrift this afternoon;
And there she shall at Friar Lawrence' cell
Be shrived and married. Here is for thy pains.

NURSE: No, truly, sir; not a penny.

ROMEO: Go to; I say you shall.

NURSE: This afternoon, sir? Well, she shall be there.

ROMEO: And stay, good nurse—behind the abbey wall
Within this hour my man shall be with thee,
And bring thee cords made like a tackled stair;
Which to the high top-gallant of my joy
Must be my convoy in the secret night.
Farewell; be trusty, and I'll quit thy pains.
Farewell; commend me to thy mistress.

NURSE: Now God in heaven bless thee!—Hark you, sir.

ROMEO: What say'st thou, my dear nurse?

NURSE: Is your man secret? Did you ne'er hear say
Two may keep counsel, putting one away?

ROMEO: I warrant thee my man's as true as steel.

NURSE: Well, sir. My mistress is the sweetest lady—Lord, Lord! when 'twas a little prating thing! O, there is a nobleman in town, one Paris, that would fain lay knife aboard; but she, good soul, had as life see a toad, a very toad, as see him. I anger her sometimes, and tell her that Paris is the properer man; but, I'll warrant you, when I say so she looks as pale as any clout in the versal world. Doth not rosemary and Romeo begin both with a letter?

ROMEO: Ay, nurse; what of that? Both with an R.

NURSE: Ah, mocker! that's the dog's name. R is for the—no, I know it begins with some other letter. And she hath the prettiest sententious of it, of you and rosemary, that it would do you good to hear it.

ROMEO: Commend me to thy lady.

NURSE: Ay, a thousand times.—Peter!

PETER: Anon.

NURSE: [*Handing him her fan*] Before and apace.

Exeunt

SCENE V—*Capulet's orchard*

Enter JULIET

JULIET: The clock struck nine when I did send the nurse;
In half an hour she promised to return.
Perchance she cannot meet him—that's not so.
O, she is lame! Love's heralds should be thoughts,
Which ten times faster glide than the sun's beams
Driving back shadows over louring hills;
Therefore do nimble-pinion'd doves draw Love,
And therefore hath the wind-swift Cupid wings.
Now is the sun upon the highmost hill
Of this day's journey; and from nine till twelve
Is three long hours, yet she is not come.
Had she affections and warm youthful blood,
She would be as swift in motion as a ball;
My words would bandy her to my sweet love,
And his to me.
But old folks—many feign as they were dead;
Unwieldy, slow, heavy, and pale as lead.

Enter Nurse and PETER

O God, she comes! O honey nurse, what news?
Hast thou met with him? Send thy man away.

NURSE: Peter, stay at the gate.

Exit PETER

JULIET: Now, good sweet nurse—O Lord, why look'st thou sad?
Though news be sad, yet tell them merrily;
If good, thou shamest the music of sweet news
By playing it to me with so sour a face.

NURSE: I am a weary, give me leave a while; Fie, how my bones ache! What a jaunu have I had!

JULIET: I would thou hadst my bones and I thy news.

Nay, come, I pray thee speak; good, good nurse, speak.
NURSE: Jesu, what haste? Can you not stay a while?
Do you not see that I am out of breath?
JULIET: How art thou out of breath, when thou hast breath
To say to me that thou art out of breath?
The excuse that thou dost make in this delay
Is longer than the tale thou dost excuse.
Is thy news good, or bad? Answer to that;
Say either, and I'll stay the circumstance.
Let me be satisfied, is't good or bad?

NURSE: Well, you have made a simple choice; you know not how to choose a man. Romeo! no, not he; though his face be better than any man's, yet his leg excels all men's; and for a hand, and a foot, and a body, though they be not to be talked on, yet they are past compare. He is not the flower of courtesy, but I'll warrant him as gentle as a lamb. Go thy ways, wench; serve God. What, have you dined at home?

JULIET: No, no. But all this did I know before.
What says he of our marriage? What of that?
NURSE: Lord, how my head aches! What a head have I!
It beats as it would fall in twenty pieces.
My back a t' other side—ah, my back, my back!
Beshrew your heart for sending me about,
To catch my death with jauncing up and down!

JULIET: I' faith, I am sorry that thou art not well. Sweet, sweet, sweet nurse, tell me, what says my love?

NURSE: Your love says like an honest gentleman, and a courteous, and a kind, and a handsome, and, I warrant, a virtuous—Where is your mother?

JULIET: Where is my mother! Why, she is within;
Where should she be? How oddly thou repliest!
'Your love says like an honest gentleman,
Where is your mother?'

NURSE: O God's lady dear!
Are you so hot? Marry, come up, I trow;
Is this the poultice for my aching bones?
Henceforward do your messages yourself.
JULIET: Here's such a coil! Come, what says Romeo?
NURSE: Have you got leave to go to shrift to-day?
JULIET: I have.
NURSE: Then hie you hence to Friar Lawrence' cell;
There stays a husband to make you a wife.
Now comes the wanton blood up in your cheeks;
They'll be in scarlet straight at any news.
Hie you to church; I must another way,
To fetch a ladder, by the which your love
Must climb a bird's nest soon when it is dark.
I am the drudge, and toil in your delight;
But you shall bear the burden soon at night.
Go; I'll to dinner; hie you to the cell.
JULIET: Hie to high fortune! Honest nurse, farewell.

Exeunt

Scene VI—*Friar Lawrence's cell*

Enter FRIAR LAWRENCE and ROMEO

FRIAR LAWRENCE: So smile the heavens upon this holy act
That after-hours with sorrow chide us not!
ROMEO: Amen, amen! But come what sorrow can,
It cannot countervail the exchange of joy
That one short minute gives me in her sight.
Do thou but close our hands with holy words,
Then love-devouring death do what he dare;
It is enough I may but call her mine.

FRIAR LAWRENCE: These violent delights have violent ends,
And in their triumph die; like fire and powder,
Which, as they kiss, consume. The sweetest honey
Is loathsome in his own deliciousness,
And in the taste confounds the appetite.
Therefore love moderately: long love doth so;
Too swift arrives as tardy as too slow.

Enter JULIET

Here comes the lady. O, so light a foot
Will ne'er wear out the everlasting flint.
A lover may bestride the gossamer
That idles in the wanton summer air
And yet not fall, so light is vanity.

JULIET: Good even to my ghostly confessor.

FRIAR LAWRENCE: Romeo shall thank thee, daughter, for us both.

JULIET: As much to him, else is his thanks too much.

ROMEO: Ah, Juliet, if the measure of thy joy
Be heap'd like mine, and that thy skill be more
To blazon it, then sweeten with thy breath
This neighbour air, and let rich music's tongue
Unfold the imagined happiness that both
Receive in either by this dear encounter.

JULIET: Conceit, more rich in matter than in words,
Brags of his substance, not of ornament.
They are but beggars that can count their worth;
But my true love is grown to such excess
I cannot sum up sum of half my wealth.

FRIAR LAWRENCE: Come, come with me, and we will make short work;
For, by your leaves, you shall not stay alone
Till holy church incorporate two in one.

Exeunt

Act III

Scene I—*A public place*

Enter MERCUTIO, BENVOLIO, Page, and Servants

BENVOLIO: I pray thee, good Mercutio, let's retire.
The day is hot, the Capulets abroad,
And if we meet we shall not scape a brawl;
For now, these hot days, is the mad blood stirring.

MERCUTIO: Thou art like one of those, fellows that when he enters the confines of a tavern, claps me his sword upon the table, and says 'God send me no need of thee!' and by the operation of the second cup draws it on the drawer, when, indeed, there is no need.

BENVOLIO: Am I like such a fellow?

MERCUTIO: Come, come, thou art as hot a Jack in thy mood as any in Italy; and as soon moved to be moody, and as soon moody to be moved.

BENVOLIO: And what to?

MERCUTIO: Nay, an there were two such, we should have none shortly, for one would kill the other. Thou! why, thou wilt quarrel with a man that hath a hair more or a hair less in his beard than thou hast. Thou wilt quarrel with a man for cracking nuts, having no other reason but because thou hast hazel eyes. What eye but such an eye would spy out such a quarrel? Thy head is as fun of quarrels as an egg is full of meat; and yet thy head hath been beaten as addle as an egg for quarrelling. Thou hast quarrelled with a man for coughing in the street, because he hath wakened thy dog that hath lain asleep in the sun. Didst thou not fall out with a tailor for wearing his new doublet before Easter? With another for tying his new shoes with old riband?

And yet thou wilt tutor me from quarrelling!

BENVOLIO: An I were so apt to quarrel as thou art, any man should buy the fee simple of my life for an hour and a quarter.

MERCUTIO: The fee simple! O simple!

Enter TYBALT and Others

BENVOLIO: By my head, here come the Capulets.

MERCUTIO: By my heel, I care not.

TYBALT: Follow me close, for I will speak to them. Gentlemen, good den; a word with one of you.

MERCUTIO: And but one word with one of us? Couple it with something; make it a word and a blow.

TYBALT: You shall find me apt enough to that, sir, an you will give me occasion.

MERCUTIO: Could you not take some occasion without giving?

TYBALT: Mercutio, thou consort'st with Romeo.

MERCUTIO: Consort! What, dost thou make us minstrels? An thou make minstrels of us, look to hear nothing but discords. Here's my fiddlestick; here's that shall make you dance. Zounds, consort!

BENVOLIO: We talk here in the public haunt of men;
Either withdraw unto some private place,
Or reason coldly of your grievances,
Or else depart; here all eyes gaze on us.

MERCUTIO: Men's eyes were made to look, and let them gaze;
I will not budge for no man's pleasure, I.

Enter ROMEO

TYBALT: Well, peace be with you, sir. Here comes my man.

MERCUTIO: But I'll be hanged, sir, if he wear your livery.
Marry, go before to field, he'll be your follower;
Your worship in that sense may call him man.

TYBALT: Romeo, the love I bear thee can afford
No better term than this: thou art a villain.

ROMEO: Tybalt, the reason that I have to love thee
Doth much excuse the appertaining rage
To such a greeting. Villain am I none;
Therefore, farewell; I see thou know'st me not.
TYBALT: Boy, this shall not excuse the injuries
That thou hast done me; therefore turn and draw.
ROMEO: I do protest I never injured thee,
But love thee better than thou canst devise
Till thou shalt know the reason of my love;
And so, good Capulet—which name I tender
As dearly as my own—be satisfied.
MERCUTIO: O calm, dishonourable, vile submission!
Alla stoccata carries it away.

Draws

Tybalt, you rat-catcher, will you walk?
TYBALT: What wouldst thou have with me?
MERCUTIO: Good King of Cats, nothing but one of your nine lives; that I mean to make bold withal, and, as you shall use me hereafter, dry-beat the rest of the eight. Will you pluck your sword out of his pilcher by the ears? Make haste, lest mine be about your ears ere it be out.
TYBALT: I am for you.

Draws

ROMEO: Gentle Mercutio, put thy rapier up.
MERCUTIO: Come, sir, your passado.

They fight

ROMEO: Draw, Benvolio; beat down their weapons.
Gentlemen, for shame, forbear this outrage!
Tybalt! Mercutio! the prince expressly hath
Forbid this bandying in Verona streets.
Hold, Tybalt! Good Mercutio!

TYBALT under ROMEO's arm thrusts MERCUTIO in and flies with his friends

MERCUTIO: I am hurt.
A plague a both your houses! I am sped.
Is he gone and hath nothing?

BENVOLIO: What, art thou hurt?

MERCUTIO: Ay, ay, a scratch, a scratch; marry, 'tis enough.
Where is my page? Go, villain, fetch a surgeon.

Exit Page

ROMEO: Courage, man; the hurt cannot be much.

MERCUTIO: No, 'tis not so deep as a well, nor so wide as a church-door; but 'tis enough,'twill serve. Ask for me to-morrow, and you shall find me a grave man. I am peppered, I warrant, for this world. A plague a both your houses! Zounds, a dog, a rat, a mouse, a cat, to scratch a man to death! A braggart, a rogue, a villain, that fights by the book of arithmetic! Why the devil came you between us? I was hurt under your arm.

ROMEO: I thought all for the best.

MERCUTIO: Help me into some house, Benvolio, or I shall faint.
A plague a both your houses!
They have made worms' meat of me.
I have it, and soundly too—your houses!

Exeunt MERCUTIO and BENVOLIO

ROMEO: This gentleman, the Prince's near ally,
My very friend, hath got his mortal hurt
In my behalf; my reputation stain'd
With Tybalt's slander—Tybalt, that an hour
Hath been my cousin. O sweet Juliet,
Thy beauty hath made me effeminate
And in my temper soften'd valour's steel!

Re-enter BENVOLIO

BENVOLIO: O Romeo, Romeo, brave Mercutio's dead!
That gallant spirit hath aspired the clouds,
Which too untimely here did scorn the earth.
ROMEO: This day's black fate on more days doth depend;
This but begins the woe others must end.

Re-enter TYBALT

BENVOLIO: Here comes the furious Tybalt back again.
ROMEO: Alive in triumph and Mercutio slain!
Away to heaven respective lenity,
And fire-eyed fury be my conduct now!
Now, Tybalt, take the 'villain' back again
That late thou gavest me; for Mercutio's soul
Is but a little way above our heads,
Staying for thine to keep him company.
Either thou or I, or both, must go with him.
TYBALT: Thou, wretched boy, that didst consort him here,
Shalt with him hence.
ROMEO: This shall determine that.

They fight; TYBALT falls

BENVOLIO: Romeo, away, be gone.
The citizens are up, and Tybalt slain.
Stand not amazed. The Prince will doom thee death
If thou art taken. Hence, be gone, away!
ROMEO: O, I am fortune's fool!
BENVOLIO: Why dost thou stay?

Exit ROMEO

Enter Citizens

FIRST CITIZEN: Which way ran he that kill'd Mercutio?
Tybalt, that murderer, which way ran he?
BENVOLIO: There lies that Tybalt.

FIRST CITIZEN: Up, sir, go with me;
I charge thee in the Prince's name, obey.

Enter Prince, attended; MONTAGUE, CAPULET, their Wives, and all

PRINCE: Where are the vile beginners of this fray?

BENVOLIO: O noble Prince, I can discover all
The unlucky manage of this fatal brawl:
There lies the man, slain by young Romeo,
That slew thy kinsman, brave Mercutio.

LADY CAPULET: Tybalt, my cousin! O my brother's child!
O Prince! O husband! O, the blood is spill'd
Of my dear kinsman! Prince, as thou art true,
For blood of ours shed blood of Montague.
O cousin, cousin!

PRINCE: Benvolio, who began this bloody fray?

BENVOLIO: Tybalt, here slain, whom Romeo's hand did slay;
Romeo that spoke him fair, bade him bethink
How nice the quarrel was, and urged withal
Your high displeasure. All this, uttered
With gentle breath, calm look, knees humbly bow'd,
Could not take truce with the unruly spleen
Of Tybalt, deaf to peace, but that he tilts
With piercing steel at bold Mercutio's breast;
Who, all as hot, turns deadly point to point,
And, with a martial scorn, with one hand beats
Cold death aside, and with the other sends
It back to Tybalt, whose dexterity
Retorts it. Romeo he cries aloud
'Hold, friends! friends, part!' and, swifter than his tongue,
His agile arm beats down their fatal points,
And 'twixt them rushes; underneath whose arm

An envious thrust from Tybalt hit the life
Of stout Mercutio; and then Tybalt fled;
But by and by comes back to Romeo,
Who had but newly entertain'd revenge,
And to't they go like lightning; for, ere I
Could draw to part them was stout Tybalt slain;
And as he fell did Romeo turn and fly.
This is the truth, or let Benvolio die.

LADY CAPULET: He is a kinsman to the Montague,
Affection makes him false, he speaks not true;
Some twenty of them fought in this black strife,
And all those twenty could but kill one life.
I beg for justice, which thou, Prince, must give:
Romeo slew Tybalt, Romeo must not live.

PRINCE: Romeo slew him; he slew Mercutio.
Who now the price of his dear blood doth owe?

MONTAGUE: Not Romeo, Prince; he was Mercutio's friend;
His fault concludes but what the law should end,
The life of Tybalt.

PRINCE: And for that offence,
Immediately we do exile him hence.
I have an interest in your hate's proceeding,
My blood for your rude brawls doth lie a-bleeding;
But I'll amerce you with so strong a fine
That you shall all repent the loss of mine.
I will be deaf to pleading and excuses,
Nor tears nor prayers shall purchase out abuses;
Therefore use none. Let Romeo hence in haste,
Else when he's found that hour is his last.
Bear hence this body, and attend our will:
Mercy but murders, pardoning those that kill.

Exeunt

Scene II—*Capulet's orchard*

Enter JULIET

JULIET: Gallop apace, you fiery-footed steeds
Towards Phœbus' lodging; such a wagoner
As Phaethon would whip you to the west,
And bring in cloudy night immediately.
Spread thy close curtain, love-performing night,
That runaways' eyes may wink, and Romeo
Leap to these arms, untalk'd of and unseen.
Lovers can see to do their amorous rites
By their own beauties; or if love be blind,
It best agrees with night. Come, civil night,
Thou sober-suited matron, all in black,
And learn me how to lose a winning match,
Play'd for a pair of stainless maidenhoods;
Hood my unmann'd blood, bating in my cheeks,
With thy black mantle, till strange love, grown bold,
Think true love acted simple modesty.
Come, night; come, Romeo; come, thou day in night;
For thou wilt lie upon the wings of night
Whiter than new snow on a raven's back.
Come, gentle night, come, loving, black-brow'd night,
Give me my Romeo; and, when he shall die,
Take him and cut him out in little stars,
And he will make the face of heaven so fine
That all the world will be in love with night,
And pay no worship to the garish sun.
O, I have bought the mansion of a love,
But not possess'd it; and, though I am sold,
Not yet enjoy'd. So tedious is this day
As is the night before some festival

To an impatient child that hath new robes,
And may not wear them. O, here comes my nurse,

Enter Nurse with cords

And she brings news; and every tongue that speaks
But Romeo's name speaks heavenly eloquence.
Now, nurse, what news? What hast thou there? The cords
That Romeo bid thee fetch?

NURSE: Ay, ay, the cords.

Throws them down

JULIET: Ay me! what news? Why dost thou wring thy hands?

NURSE: Ah, well-a-day! he's dead, he's dead, he's dead.
We are undone, lady, we are undone.
Alack the day! he's gone, he's kill'd, he's dead.

JULIET: Can heaven be so envious?

NURSE: Romeo can,
Though heaven cannot. O Romeo, Romeo!
Who ever would have thought it? Romeo!

JULIET: What devil art thou that dost torment me thus?
This torture should be roar'd in dismal hell.
Hath Romeo slain himself? Say thou but 'I',
And that bare vowel I shall poison more
Than the death-darting eye of cockatrice.
I am not I if there be such an 'I';
Or those eyes shut that make thee answer 'I'.
If he be slain, say 'I'; or if not, 'No';
Brief sounds determine of my weal or woe.

NURSE: I saw the wound, I saw it with mine eyes—
God save the mark!—here on his manly breast.
A piteous corse, a bloody piteous corse;
Pale, pale as ashes, all bedaub'd in blood,
All in gore-blood. I swounded at the sight.

JULIET: O, break, my heart! poor bankrupt, break at once!
To prison, eyes; ne'er look on liberty.
Vile earth, to earth resign; end motion here;
And thou and Romeo press one heavy bier!
NURSE: O Tybalt, Tybalt, the best friend I had!
O courteous Tybalt! honest gentleman!
That ever I should live to see thee dead!
JULIET: What storm is this that blows so contrary?
Is Romeo slaughter'd, and is Tybalt dead?
My dearest cousin and my dearer lord?
Then, dreadful trumpet, sound the general doom;
For who is living if those two are gone?
NURSE: Tybalt is gone, and Romeo banished;
Romeo that kill'd him, he is banished.
JULIET: O God! Did Romeo's hand shed Tybalt's blood?
NURSE: It did, it did; alas the day, it did!
JULIET: O serpent heart, hid with a flowering face!
Did ever dragon keep so fair a cave?
Beautiful tyrant! fiend angelical!
Dove-feather'd raven! wolfish-ravening lamb!
Despised substance of divinest show!
Just opposite to what thou justly seem'st,
A damned saint, an honourable villain!
O nature, what hadst thou to do in hell,
When thou didst bower the spirit of a fiend
In moral paradise of such sweet flesh?
Was ever book containing such vile matter
So fairly bound? O, that deceit should dwell
In such a gorgeous palace!
NURSE: There's no trust,
No faith, no honesty in men; all perjured,
All forsworn, all naught, all dissemblers.

Ah, where's my man? Give me some aqua vitæ:
These griefs, these woes, these sorrows, make me old.
Shame come to Romeo!

JULIET: Blister'd be thy tongue
For such a wish! He was not born to shame:
Upon his brow shame is ashamed to sit;
For 'tis a throne where honour may be crown'd
Sole monarch of the universal earth.
O, what a beast was I to chide at him!

NURSE: Will you speak well of him that kill'd your cousin?

JULIET: Shall I speak ill of him that is my husband?
Ah, poor my lord, what tongue shall smooth thy name,
When I, thy three-hours wife, have mangled it?
But wherefore, villain, didst thou kill my cousin?
That villain cousin would have kill'd my husband.
Back, foolish tears, back to your native spring;
Your tributary drops belong to woe,
Which you, mistaking, offer up to joy.
My husband lives that Tybalt would have slain,
And Tybalt's dead, that would have slain my husband.
All this is comfort; wherefore weep I then?
Some word there was, worser than Tybalt's death,
That murder'd me; I would forget it fain,
But, O, it presses to my memory
Like damned guilty deeds to sinners' minds:
'Tybalt is dead, and Romeo banished';
That 'banished', that one word 'banished',
Hath slain ten thousand Tybalts. Tybalt's death
Was woe enough, if it had ended there;
Or if sour woe delights in fellowship
And needly will be rank'd with other griefs,
Why follow'd not, when she said 'Tybalt's dead',

Thy father or thy mother, nay, or both,
Which modern lamentations might have moved?
But, with a rear-ward following Tybalt's death,
'Romeo is banished'—to speak that word
Is father, mother, Tybalt, Romeo, Juliet,
All slain, all dead. 'Romeo is banished'—
There is no end, no limit, measure, bound,
In that word's death; no words can that woe sound.
Where is my father and my mother, nurse?
NURSE: Weeping and wailing over Tybalt's corse.
Will you go to them? I will bring you thither.
JULIET: Wash they his wounds with tears! Mine shall be spent,
When theirs are dry, for Romeo's banishment.
Take up those cords. Poor ropes, you are beguiled,
Both you and I, for Romeo is exiled;
He made you for a highway to my bed,
But I, a maid, die maiden-widowed.
Come, cords; come, nurse; I'll to my wedding-bed;
And death, not Romeo, take my maidenhead!
NURSE: Hie to your chamber; I'll find Romeo
To comfort you. I wot well where he is.
Hark ye, your Romeo will be here at night.
I'll to him; he is hid at Laurence' cell.
JULIET: O, find him! give this ring to my true knight,
And bid him come to take his last farewell.

Exeunt

Scene III—*Friar Lawrence's cell*

Enter FRIAR LAWRENCE

FRIAR LAWRENCE: Romeo, come forth; come forth, thou fearful man

Affliction is enamour'd of thy parts,
And thou art wedded to calamity.

Enter ROMEO

ROMEO: Father, what news? What is the Prince's doom?
What sorrow craves acquaintance at my hand,
That I yet know not?
FRIAR LAWRENCE: Too familiar
Is my dear son with such sour company;
I bring thee tidings of the Prince's doom.
ROMEO: What less than dooms day is the Prince's doom?
FRIAR LAWRENCE: A gentler judgment vanish'd from his lips—
Not body's death, but body's banishment.
ROMEO: Ha, banishment! Be merciful, say 'death';
For exile hath more terror in his look,
Much more than death: Do not say 'banishment'.
FRIAR LAWRENCE: Hence from Verona art thou banished.
Be patient, for the world is broad and wide.
ROMEO: There is no world without Verona walls,
But purgatory, torture, hell itself.
Hence banished is banish'd from the world,
And world's exile is death. Then 'banished',
Is death mis-term'd calling death; 'banishment',
Thou cut'st my head off with a golden axe,
And smilest upon the stroke that murders me.
FRIAR LAWRENCE: O deadly sin! O rude unthankfulness!
Thy fault our law calls death; but the kind Prince,
Taking thy part, hath rush'd aside the law,
And turn'd that black word death to banishment.
This is dear mercy, and thou seest it not.
ROMEO: 'Tis torture, and not mercy; heaven is here
Where Juliet lives, and every cat, and dog,
And little mouse, every unworthy thing,

Live here in heaven and may look on her;
But Romeo may not. More validity,
More honourable state, more courtship lives
In carrion flies than Romeo. They my seize
On the white wonder of dear Juliet's hand,
And steal immortal blessing from her lips;
Who, even in pure and vestal modesty,
Still blush, as thinking their own kisses sin;
But Romeo may not—he is banished.
This may flies do, when I from this must fly;
They are free men, but I am banished.
And say'st thou yet that exile is not death?
Hadst thou no poison mix'd, no sharp-ground knife,
No sudden mean of death, though ne'er so mean,
But 'banished' to kill me—'banished'?
O friar, the damned use that word in hell;
Howling attends it; how hast thou the heart,
Being a divine, a ghostly confessor,
A sin-absolver, and my friend profess'd,
To mangle me with that word 'banished'?
FRIAR LAWRENCE: Thou fond mad man, hear me a little speak.
ROMEO: O, thou wilt speak again of banishment.
FRIAR LAWRENCE: I'll give thee armour to keep off that word;
Adversity's sweet milk, philosophy,
To comfort thee, though thou art banished.
ROMEO: Yet 'banished'? Hang up philosophy;
Unless philosophy can make a Juliet,
Displant a town, reverse a prince's doom,
It helps not, it prevails not. Talk no more.
FRIAR LAWRENCE: O, then I see that madmen have no ears.
ROMEO: How should they, when that wise men have no eyes?
FRIAR LAWRENCE: Let me dispute with thee of thy estate.

ROMEO: Thou canst not speak of that thou dost not feel.
Wert thou as young as I, Juliet thy love,
An hour but married, Tybalt murdered,
Doting like me, and like me banished,
Then mightst thou speak, then mightst thou tear thy hair,
And fall upon the ground, as I do now,
Taking the measure of an unmade grave.

Knocking within

FRIAR LAWRENCE: Arise; one knocks. Good Romeo, hide thyself.

ROMEO: Not I; unless the breath of heartsick groans,
Mist-like, enfold me from the search of eyes.

Knocking

FRIAR LAWRENCE: Hark how they knock! Who's there? Romeo, arise;
Thou wilt be taken—Stay awhile.—Stand up;

Knocking

Run to my study—By and by.—God's will,
What simpleness is this!—I come, I come.

Knocking

Who knocks so hard? Whence come you? What's your will?

NURSE: [*Within*] Let me come in and you shall know my errand;
I come from Lady Juliet.

FRIAR LAWRENCE: Welcome, then.

Enter Nurse

NURSE: O holy friar, O, tell me, holy friar,
Where is my lady's lord, where's Romeo?

FRIAR LAWRENCE: There on the ground, with his own tears made drunk.

NURSE: O, he is even in my mistress' case,
Just in her case!

FRIAR LAWRENCE: O woeful sympathy!
Piteous predicament!
NURSE: Even so lies she,
Blubbering and weeping, weeping and blubbering.
Stand up, stand up; stand, an you be a man;
For Juliet's sake, for her sake, rise and stand;
Why should you fall into so deep an O?
ROMEO: Nurse!
NURSE: Ah, sir! Ah, sir! Well, death's the end of all.
ROMEO: Spakest thou of Juliet? How is it with her?
Doth not she think me an old murderer,
Now I have stain'd the childhood of our joy
With blood removed but little from her own?
Where is she? and how doth she? and what says
My conceal'd lady to our cancell'd love?
NURSE: O, she says nothing, sir, but weeps and weeps;
And now falls on her bed, and then starts up,
And Tybalt calls; and then on Romeo cries,
And then down falls again.
ROMEO: As if that name,
Shot from the deadly level of a gun,
Did murder her; as that name's cursed hand
Murder'd her kinsman. O, tell me, friar, tell me,
In what vile part of this anatomy
Doth my name lodge? Tell me that I may sack
The hateful mansion.

Drawing his sword

FRIAR LAWRENCE: Hold thy desperate hand.
Art thou a man? Thy form cries out thou art:
Thy tears are womanish; thy wild acts denote
The unreasonable fury of a beast.
Unseemly woman in a seeming man!

And ill-beseeming beast in seeming both!
Thou hast amazed me. By my holy order,
I thought thy disposition better temper'd.
Hast thou slain Tybalt? Wilt thou slay thyself?
And slay thy lady that in thy life lives,
By doing damned hate upon thyself?
Why rail'st thou on thy birth, the heaven, and earth?
Since birth, and heaven, and earth, all three do meet
In thee at once; which thou at once wouldst lose.
Fie, fie! thou shamest thy shape, thy love, thy wit;
Which, like a usurer, abound'st in all,
And usest none in that true use indeed
Which should bedeck thy shape, thy love, thy wit.
Thy noble shape is but a form of wax,
Digressing from the valour of a man;
Thy dear love sworn but hollow perjury,
Killing that love which thou hast vow'd to cherish;
Thy wit, that ornament to shape and love,
Misshapen in the conduct of them both,
Like powder in a skitless soldier's flask,
Is set afire by thine own ignorance,
And thou dismember'd with thine own defence.
What, rouse thee, man! Thy Juliet is alive,
For whose dear sake thou wast but lately dead;
There art thou happy. Tybalt would kill thee,
But thou slew'st Tybalt; there are thou happy too.
The law that threaten'd death, becomes thy friend,
And turns it to exile; there art thou happy.
A pack of blessings lights up upon thy back;
Happiness courts thee in her best array;
But, like a misbehaved and sullen wench,
Thou pout'st upon thy fortune and thy love.

Take heed, take heed, for such die miserable.
Go, get thee to thy love, as was decreed,
Ascend her chamber, hence and comfort her:
But look thou stay not till the watch be set,
For then thou canst not pass to Mantua,
Where thou shalt live till we can find a time
To blaze your marriage, reconcile your friends,
Beg pardon of the Prince, and call thee back
With twenty hundred thousand times more joy
Than thou went'st forth in lamentation.
Go before, nurse; commend me to thy lady;
And bid her hasten all the house to bed,
Which heavy sorrow makes them apt unto;
Romeo is coming.

NURSE: O Lord, I could have stay'd here all the night
To hear good counsel; O, what learning is!
My lord, I'll tell my lady you will come.

ROMEO: Do so, and bid my sweet prepare to chide.

NURSE: Here, sir, a ring she bid me give you, sir.
Hie you, make haste, for it grows very late.

Exit

ROMEO: How well my comfort is revived by this!

FRIAR LAWRENCE: Go hence; good night; and here stands all your state:
Either be gone before the watch be set,
Or by the break of day disguised from hence.
Sojourn in Mantua; I'll find out your man,
And he shall signify from time to time
Every good hap to you that chances here.
Give me thy hand. 'Tis late; farewell; good night.

ROMEO: But that a joy past joy calls out on me,

It were a grief so brief to part with thee
Farewell.

Exeunt

Scene IV—*Capulet's house*

Enter CAPULET, LADY CAPULET, and PARIS

CAPULET: Things have fall'n out, sir, so unluckily
That we have had no time to move our daughter.
Look you, she loved her kinsman Tybalt dearly,
And so did I. Well, we were born to die.
'Tis very late, she'll not come down to-night.
I promise you, but for your company,
I would have been a bed an hour ago.

PARIS: These times of woe afford no time to woo.
Madam, good night; commend me to your daughter.

LADY CAPULET: I will, and know her mind early to-morrow;
To-night she is mew'd up to her heaviness.

CAPULET: Sir Paris, I will make a desperate tender
Of my child's love. I think she will be ruled
In all respects by me; nay, more, I doubt it not.
Wife, go you to her ere you go to bed;
Acquaint her here of my son Paris' love
And bid her, mark you me, on Wednesday next—
But, soft! what day is this?

PARIS: Monday, my lord.

CAPULET: Monday! ha, ha! Well, Wednesday is too soon.
A Thursday let it be: a Thursday, tell her,
She shall be married to this noble earl.
Will you be ready? Do you like this haste?
We'll keep no great ado—a friend or two;

For, hark you, Tybalt being slain so late,
It may be thought we held him carelessly,
Being our kinsman, if we revel much;
Therefore we'll have some half a dozen friends,
And there an end. But what say you to Thursday?
PARIS: My lord, I would that Thursday were to-morrow.
CAPULET: Well, get you gone: a Thursday be it then.
Go you to Juliet ere you go to bed;
Prepare her, wife, against this wedding-day.
Farewell, my lord. Light to my chamber, ho!
Afore me, it is so very very late
That we may call it early by and by.
Good night.

Exeunt

Scene V—*Capulet's orchard*

Enter ROMEO and JULIET, aloft
JULIET: Wilt thou be gone? It is not yet near day;
It was the nightingale, and not the lark,
That pierced the fearful hollow of thine ear;
Nightly she sings on yond pomegranate tree.
Believe me, love, it was the nightingale.
ROMEO: It was the lark, the herald of the morn,
No nightingale. Look, love, what envious streaks
Do lace the severing clouds in yonder east;
Night's candles are burnt out, and jocund day
Stands tiptoe on the misty mountain tops.
I must be gone and live, or stay and die.
JULIET: Yond light is not day light; I know it, I:
It is some meteor that the sun exhales
To be to thee this night a torch-bearer,

And light thee on thy way to Mantua;
Therefore stay yet; thou need'st not to be gone.
ROMEO: Let me be ta'en, let me be put to death;
I am content, so thou wilt have it so.
I'll say yon grey is not the morning's eye,
'Tis but the pale reflex of Cynthia's brow;
Nor that is not the lark whose notes do beat
The vaulty heaven so high above our heads.
I have more care to stay than will to go.
Come death, and welcome! Juliet wills it so.
How is't, my soul? Let's talk—it is not day.
JULIET: It is, it is; hie hence, be gone, away!
It is the lark that sings so out of tune,
Straining harsh discords and unpleasing sharps.
Some say the lark makes sweet division;
This doth not so, for she divideth us.
Some say the lark and loathed toad change eyes;
O, now I would they had changed voices too!
Since arm from arm that voice doth us affray,
Hunting thee hence with hunts-up to the day.
O, now be gone! More light and light it grows.
ROMEO: More light and light—more dark and dark our woes!

Enter Nurse

NURSE: Madam!
JULIET: Nurse?
NURSE: Your lady mother is coming to your chamber.
The day is broke; be wary, look about.

Exit

JULIET: Then, window, let day in and let life out.
ROMEO: Farewell, farewell! One kiss, and I'll descend.

He goeth down

JULIET: Art thou gone so, love—lord, ay, husband, friend!
I must hear from thee every day in the hour,
For in a minute there are many days;
O, by this count I shall be much in years
Ere I again behold my Romeo!

ROMEO: Farewell!
I will omit no opportunity
That may convey my greetings, love, to thee.

JULIET: O think'st thou we shall ever meet again?

ROMEO: I doubt it not; and all these woes shall serve
For sweet discourses in our time to come.

JULIET: O God, I have an ill-divining soul!
Methinks I see thee, now thou art below,
As one dead in the bottom of a tomb:
Either my eyesight fails, or thou look'st pale.

ROMEO: And trust me, love, in my eye so do you:
Dry sorrow drinks our blood. Adieu, adieu!

Exit below

JULIET: O Fortune, Fortune! all men call thee fickle.
If thou art fickle, what dost thou with him
That is renown'd for faith? Be fickle, Fortune;
For then, I hope, thou wilt not keep him long,
But send him back.

LADY CAPULET: [*Within*] Ho, daughter! are you up?

JULIET: Who is't that calls? It is my lady mother.
Is she not down so late, or up so early?
What unaccustom'd cause procures her hither?

Enter LADY CAPULET

LADY CAPULET: Why, how now, Juliet!

JULIET: Madam, I am not well.

LADY CAPULET: Evermore weeping for your cousin's death?

What, wilt thou wash him from his grave with tears?
An if thou couldst, thou couldst not make him live;
Therefore have done. Some grief shows much of love;
But much of grief shows still some want of wit.

JULIET: Yet let me weep for such a feeling loss.

LADY CAPULET: So shall you feel the loss, but not the friend
Which you weep for.

JULIET: Feeling so the loss,
I cannot choose but ever weep the friend.

LADY CAPULET: Well, girl, thou weep'st not so much for his death
As that the villain lives which slaughter'd him.

JULIET: What villain, madam?

LADY CAPULET: That same villain, Romeo.

JULIET: [*Aside*] Villain and he be many miles asunder!—
God pardon him! I do, with all my heart;
And yet no man like he doth grieve my heart.

LADY CAPULET: That is because the traitor murderer lives.

JULIET: Ay, madam, from the reach of these my hands.
Would none but I might venge my cousin's death!

LADY CAPULET: We will have vengeance for it, fear thou not;
Then weep no more. I'll send to one in Mantua—
Where that same banish'd runagate doth live—
Shall give him such an unaccustom'd dram
That he shall soon keep Tybalt company;
And then I hope thou wilt be satisfied.

JULIET: Indeed I never shall be satisfied
With Romeo, till I behold him—dead—
Is my poor heart so for a kinsman vex'd.
Madam, if you could find out but a man
To bear a poison, I would temper it,
That Romeo should, upon receipt thereof,

Soon sleep in quiet. O, how my heart abhors
To hear him named, and cannot come to him,
To wreak the love I bore my cousin Tybalt
Upon his body that slaughter'd him!

LADY CAPULET: Find thou the means, and I'll find such a man.
But now I'll tell thee joyful tidings, girl.

JULIET: And joy comes well in such a needy time.
What are they, beseech your ladyship?

LADY CAPULET: Well, well, thou hast a careful father, child;
One who, to put thee from thy heaviness,
Hath sorted out a sudden day of joy
That thou expect'st not, nor I look'd not for.

JULIET: Madam, in happy time, what day is that?

LADY CAPULET: Marry, my child, early next Thursday morn
The gallant, young, and noble gentleman,
The County Paris, at Saint Peter's Church,
Shall happily make thee there a joyful bride.

JULIET: Now, by Saint Peter's Church, and Peter too,
He shall not make me there a joyful bride.
I wonder at this haste, that I must wed
Ere he that should be husband comes to woo.
I pray you tell my lord and father, madam,
I will not marry yet; and, when I do, I swear,
It shall be Romeo, whom you know I hate,
Rather than Paris. These are news indeed!

LADY CAPULET: Here comes your father; tell him so yourself,
And see how he will take it at your hands.

Enter CAPULET and Nurse

CAPULET: When the sun sets, the air doth drizzle dew;
But for the sunset of my brother's son
It rains downright.
How now! a conduit, girl? What, still in tears?

Evermore showering? In one little body
Thou counterfeit'st a bark, a sea, a wind;
For still thy eyes, which I may call the sea,
Do ebb and flow with tears. The bark thy body is,
Sailing in this salt flood; the winds thy sighs,
Who, raging with thy tears, and they with them,
Without a sudden calm will overset
Thy tempest-tossed body. How now, wife!
Have you deliver'd to her our decree?

LADY CAPULET: Ay, sir; but she will none, she gives you thanks.
I would the fool were married to her grave!

CAPULET: Soft! take me with you, take me with you, wife.
How will she none? Doth she not give us thanks?
Is she not proud? Doth she not count her blest,
Unworthy as she is, that we have wrought
So worthy a gentleman to be her bridegroom?

JULIET: Not proud you have, but thankful that you have.
Proud can I never be of what I hate,
But thankful even for hate that is meant love.

CAPULET: How how, how how, chopt logic! What is this?
'Proud,' and 'I thank you,' and 'I thank you not'—
And yet 'not proud'? Mistress minion, you,
Thank me no thankings, nor proud me no prouds,
But fettle your fine joints 'gainst Thursday next,
To go with Paris to Saint Peter's Church,
Or I will drag thee on a hurdle thither.
Out, you green-sickness carrion! Out, you baggage!
You tallow-face!

LADY CAPULET: Fie, fie! what, are you mad?

JULIET: Good father, I beseech you on my knees,
Hear me with patience but to speak a word.

CAPULET: Hang thee, young baggage! disobedient wretch!
I tell thee what—get thee to church a Thursday,
Or never after look me in the face.
Speak not, reply not, do not answer me;
My fingers itch. Wife, we scarce thought us blest
That God had lent us but this only child;
But now I see this one is one too much,
And that we have a curse in having her.
Out on her, hilding!
NURSE: God in heaven bless her!
You are to blame, my lord, to rate her so.
CAPULET: And why, my Lady Wisdom? Hold your tongue,
Good Prudence; smatter with your gossips, go.
NURSE: I speak no treason.
CAPULET: O, God-i-goden!
NURSE: May not one speak?
CAPULET: Peace, you mumbling fool!
Utter your gravity o'er a gossip's bowl,
For here we need it not.
LADY CAPULET: You are too hot.
CAPULET: God's bread! it makes me mad:
Day, night, hour, tide, time, work, play,
Alone, in company, still my care hath been
To have her match'd; and having now provided
A gentleman of noble parentage,
Of fair demesnes, youthful, and nobly train'd,
Stuff'd, as they say, with honourable parts,
Proportion'd as one's thought would wish a man—
And then to have a wretched puling fool,
A whining mammet, in her fortune's tender,
To answer 'I'll not wed, I cannot love,
I am too young, I pray you pardon me'!

But, as you will not wed, I'll pardon you.
Graze where you will, you shall not house with me.
Look to 't, think on't, I do not use to jest.
Thursday is near; lay hand on heart, advise:
An you be mine, I'll give you to my friend;
An you be not, hang, beg, starve, die in the streets,
For, by my soul, I'll ne'er acknowledge thee,
Nor what is mine shall never do thee good.
Trust to't, bethink you, I'll not be forsworn.

Exit

JULIET: Is there no pity sitting in the clouds
That sees into the bottom of my grief?
O, sweet my mother, cast me not away!
Delay this marriage for a month, a week;
Or, if you do not, make the bridal bed
In that dim monument where Tybalt lies.

LADY CAPULET: Talk not to me, for I'll not speak a word;
Do as thou wilt, for I have done with thee.

Exit

JULIET: O God!—O nurse! how shall this be prevented?
My husband is on earth, my faith in heaven;
How shall that faith return again to earth,
Unless that husband send it me from heaven
By leaving earth? Comfort me, counsel me.
Alack, alack, that heaven should practise stratagems
Upon so soft a subject as myself!
What say'st thou? Hast thou not a word of joy?
Some comfort, nurse.

NURSE: Faith, here it is:
Romeo is banish'd; and all the world to nothing
That he dares ne'er come back to challenge you;

Or, if he do, it needs must be by stealth.
Then, since the case so stands as now it doth,
I think it best you married with the County.
O, he's a lovely gentleman!
Romeo's a dishclout to him; an eagle, madam,
Hath not so green, so quick, so fair an eye
As Paris hath. Beshrew my very heart,
I think you are happy in this second match,
For it excels your first; or if it did not,
Your first is dead, or 'twere as good he were
As living here and you no use of him.

JULIET: Speakest thou from thy heart?

NURSE: And from my soul too, else beshrew them both.

JULIET: Amen!

NURSE: What?

JULIET: Well, thou hast comforted me marvellous much.
Go in; and tell my lady I am gone,
Having displeased my father, to Laurence' cell
To make confession, and to be absolved.

NURSE: Marry, I will; and this is wisely done.

Exit

JULIET: Ancient damnation! O most wicked fiend!
Is it more sin to wish me thus forsworn,
Or to dispraise my lord with that same tongue
Which she hath praised him with above compare
So many thousand times? Go, counsellor;
Thou and my bosom henceforth shall be twain.
I'll to the friar to know his remedy;
If all else fail, myself have power to die.

Exit

Act IV

Scene I—*Friar Lawrence's cell*

Enter FRIAR LAWRENCE and COUNTY PARIS

FRIAR LAWRENCE: On Thursday, sir? The time is very short.

PARIS: My father Capulet will have it so,
And I am nothing slow to slack his haste.

FRIAR LAWRENCE: You say you do not know the lady's mind;
Uneven is the course; I like it not.

PARIS: Immoderately she weeps for Tybalt's death,
And therefore have I little talk'd of love;
For Venus smiles not in a house of tears.
Now, sir, her father counts it dangerous
That she doth give her sorrow so much sway,
And in his wisdom hastes our marriage,
To stop the inundation of her tears;
Which, too much minded by herself alone,
May be put from her by society.
Now do you know the reason of this haste.

FRIAR LAWRENCE: [*Aside*] I would I knew not why it should be slow'd.
Look, sir, here comes the lady toward my cell.

Enter JULIET

PARIS: Happily met, my lady and my wife!

JULIET: That may be, sir, when I may be a wife.

PARIS: That may be must be, love, on Thursday next.

JULIET: What must be shall be.

FRIAR LAWRENCE: That's a certain text.

PARIS: Come you to make confession to this father?
JULIET: To answer that, I should confess to you.
PARIS: Do not deny to him that you love me.
JULIET: I will confess to you that I love him.
PARIS: So will ye, I am sure, that you love me.
JULIET: If I do so, it will be of more price
Being spoke behind your back than to your face.
PARIS: Poor soul, thy face is much abused with tears.
JULIET: The tears have got small victory by that,
For it was bad enough before their spite.
PARIS: Thou wrong'st it more than tears with that report.
JULIET: That is no slander, sir, which is a truth;
And what I spake, I spake it to my face.
PARIS: Thy face is mine, and thou hast slander'd it.
JULIET: It may be so, for it is not mine own,
Are you at leisure, holy father, now;
Or shall I come to you at evening mass?
FRIAR LAWRENCE: My leisure serves me, pensive daughter, now.
My lord, we must entreat the time alone.
PARIS: God shield I should disturb devotion!
Juliet, on Thursday early will I rouse ye;
Till then, adieu, and keep this holy kiss.

Exit

JULIET: O, shut the door, and when thou hast done so,
Come weep with me—past hope, past cure, past help.
FRIAR LAWRENCE: O, Juliet, I already know thy grief;
It strains me past the compass of my wits.
I hear thou must, and nothing may prorogue it,
On Thursday next be married to this County.

JULIET: Tell me not, friar, that thou hear'st of this,
Unless thou tell me how I may prevent it,
If, in thy wisdom, thou canst give no help,
Do thou but call my resolution wise,
And with this knife I'll help it presently.
God join'd my heart and Romeo's, thou our hands;
And ere this hand, by thee to Romeo seal'd,
Shall be the label to another deed,
Or my true heart with treacherous revolt
Turn to another, this shall slay them both.
Therefore, out of thy long-experienced time,
Give me some present counsel; or, behold,
'Twixt my extremes and me this bloody knife
Shall play the umpire, arbitrating that
Which the commission of thy years and art
Could to no issue of true honour bring.
Be not so long to speak; I long to die,
If what thou speak'st speak not of remedy.

FRIAR LAWRENCE: Hold, daughter; I do spy a kind of hope,
Which craves as desperate an execution
As that is desperate which we would prevent.
If, rather than to marry County Paris,
Thou hast the strength of will to slay thyself,
Then is it likely thou wilt undertake
A thing like death to chide away this shame,
That copest with death himself to scape from it;
And, if thou darest, I'll give thee remedy.

JULIET: O, bid me leap, rather than marry Paris,
From off the battlements of any tower,
Or walk in thievish ways, or bid me lurk
Where serpents are; chain me with roaring bears,
Or hide me nightly in a charnel house,

O'er-cover'd quite with dead men's rattling bones,
With reeky shanks and yellow chapless skulls;
Or bid me go into a new-made grave,
And hide me with a dead man in his shroud—
Things that, to hear them told, have made me tremble—
And I will do it without fear or doubt,
To live an unstain'd wife to my sweet love.
FRIAR LAWRENCE: Hold, then; go home, be merry, give consent
To marry Paris. Wednesday is to-morrow;
To-morrow night look that thou lie alone,
Let not the nurse lie with thee in thy chamber.
Take thou this vial, being then in bed,
And this distilled liquor drink thou off;
When presently through all thy veins shall run
A cold and drowsy humour; for no pulse
Shall keep his native progress, but surcease;
No warmth, no breath, shall testify thou livest;
The roses in thy lips and cheeks shall fade
To paly ashes, thy eyes' windows fall,
Like death, when he shuts up the day of life;
Each part, deprived of supple government,
Shall, stiff and stark and cold, appear like death;
And in this borrow'd likeness of shrunk death
Thou shalt continue two and forty hours,
And then awake as from a pleasant sleep.
Now, when the bridegroom in the morning comes
To rouse thee from thy bed, there art thou dead.
Then, as the manner of our country is,
In thy best robes, uncover'd on the bier,
Thou shalt be borne to that same ancient vault
Where all the kindred of the Capulets lie.
In the meantime, against thou shalt awake,

Shall Romeo by my letters know our drift,
And hither shall he come; and he and I
Will watch thy waking, and that very night
Shall Romeo bear thee hence to Mantua.
And this shall free thee from this present shame,
If no inconstant toy nor womanish fear
Abate thy valour in the acting it.

JULIET: Give me, give me! O, tell not me of fear!

FRIAR LAWRENCE: Hold; get you gone, be strong and prosperous
In this resolve. I'll send a friar with speed
To Mantua, with my letters to thy lord.

JULIET: Love give me strength! and strength shall help afford.
Farewell, dear father!

Exeunt

SCENE II—*Capulet's house*

Enter CAPULET, LADY CAPULET, Nurse, and two or three Servingmen

CAPULET: So many guests invite as here are writ.

Exit a Servingman

Sirrah, go hire me twenty cunning cooks.

SERVINGMAN: You shall have none ill, sir; for I'll try if they can lick their fingers.

CAPULET: How canst thou try them so?

SERVINGMAN: Marry, sir, 'tis an ill cook that cannot lick his own fingers; therefore he that cannot lick his fingers goes not with me.

CAPULET: Go, be gone.

Exit Second Servingman

We shall be much unfurnished for this time.
What, is my daughter gone to Friar Lawrence?

NURSE: Ay, forsooth.

CAPULET: Well, he may chance to do some good on her:
A peevish self-will'd harlotry it is.

Enter JULIET

NURSE: See where she comes from shrift with merry look.

CAPULET: How now, my headstrong! Where have you been gadding?

JULIET: Where I have learnt me to repent the sin
Of disobedient opposition
To you and your behests; and am enjoin'd
By holy Lawrence to fall prostrate here
To beg your pardon. Pardon, I beseech you.
Henceforward I am ever ruled by you.

CAPULET: Send for the County; go tell him of this.
I'll have this knot knit up to-morrow morning.

JULIET: I met the youthful lord at Lawrence' cell,
And gave him what becomed love I might,
Not stepping o'er the bounds of modesty.

CAPULET: Why, I am glad on't; this is well—stand up—
This is as't should be. Let me see the County;
Ay, marry, go, I say, and fetch him hither.
Now, afore God, this reverend holy friar,
All our whole city is much bound to him.

JULIET: Nurse, will you go with me into my closet
To help me sort such needful ornaments
As you think fit to furnish me to-morrow?

LADY CAPULET: No, not till Thursday; there is time enough.

CAPULET: Go, nurse, go with her. We'll to church to-morrow.

Exeunt JULIET and Nurse

LADY CAPULET: We shall be short in our provision:
'Tis now near night.

CAPULET: Tush, I will stir about,
And all things shall be well, I warrant thee, wife.
Go thou to Juliet, help to deck up her;
I'll not to bed to-night; let me alone.
I'll play the housewife for this once. What, ho!
They are all forth; well, I will walk myself
To County Paris, to prepare up him
Against to-morrow. My heart is wondrous light
Since this same wayward girl is so reclaim'd.

Exeunt

SCENE III—*Juliet's chamber*

Enter JULIET and Nurse

JULIET: Ay, those attires are best; but, gentle nurse,
I pray thee, leave me to myself to-night,
For I have need of many orisons
To move the heavens to smile upon my state,
Which well thou know'st is cross and full of sin.

Enter LADY CAPULET

LADY CAPULET: What, are you busy, ho? Need you my help?
JULIET: No, madam; we have cull'd such necessaries
As are behoveful for our state to-morrow.
So please you, let me now be left alone,
And let the nurse this night sit up with you;
For I am sure you have your hands full all
In this so sudden business.
LADY CAPULET: Good night.
Get thee to bed, and rest; for thou hast need.

Exeunt LADY CAPULET and Nurse

JULIET: Farewell! God knows when we shall meet again.
I have a faint cold fear thrills through my veins,
That almost freezes up the heat of life;
I'll call them back again to comfort me.
Nurse!—What should she do here?
My dismal scene I needs must act alone. Come, vial.
What if this mixture do not work at all?
Shall I be married, then to-morrow morning?
No, no; this shall forbid it. Lie thou there.

Laying down her dagger

What if it be a poison which the friar
Subtly hath minister'd to have me dead,
Lest in this marriage he should be dishonour'd,
Because he married me before to Romeo?
I fear it is; and yet methinks it should not,
For he hath still been tried a holy man.
How if, when I am laid into the tomb,
I wake before the time that Romeo
Come to redeem me? There's a fearful point.
Shall I not then be stifled in the vault,
To whose foul mouth no healthsome air breathes in,
And there die strangled ere my Romeo comes?
Or, if I live, is it not very like
The horrible conceit of death and night,
Together with the terror of the place—
As in a vault, an ancient receptacle
Where for these many hundred years the bones
Of all my buried ancestors are packed;
Where bloody Tybalt, yet but green in earth,
Lies festering in his shroud; where, as they say,
At some hours in the night spirits resort—
Alack, alack, is it not like that I,

So early waking—what with loathsome smells,
And shrieks like mandrakes' torn out of the earth,
That living mortals, hearing them, run mad—
O, if I wake, shall I not be distraught,
Environed with all these hideous fears,
And madly play with my forefather's joints,
And pluck the mangled Tybalt from his shroud,
And, in this rage, with some great kinsman's bone,
As with a club, dash out my desperate brains?
O, look! methinks I see my cousin's ghost
Seeking out Romeo, that did spit his body
Upon a rapier's point. Stay, Tybalt, stay.
Romeo, I come. This do I drink to thee.

She drinks and falls upon her bed, within the curtains

Scene IV—*Capulet's house*

Enter LADY CAPULET and Nurse

LADY CAPULET: Hold, take these keys, and fetch more spices, nurse.

NURSE: They call for dates and quinces in the pastry.

Enter CAPULET

CAPULET: Come, stir, stir, stir! The second cock. hath crow'd,
The curfew-bell hath rung, 'tis three o'clock:
Look to the baked meats, good Angelica;
Spare not for the cost.

NURSE: Go, you cot-quean, go,
Get you to bed; faith, You'll be sick to-morrow
For this night's watching.

CAPULET: No, not a whit; what! I have watch'd ere now
All night for lesser cause, and ne'er been sick.

LADY CAPULET: Ay, you have been a mouse-hunt in your time;
But I will watch you from such watching now.

Exeunt LADY CAPULET and Nurse

CAPULET: A jealous hood, a jealous hood!

Enter three or four Servingmen with spits and logs and baskets

Now, fellow,
What's there?

FIRST FELLOW: Things for the cook, sir; but I know not what.

CAPULET: Make haste, make haste.

Exit First Fellow

Sirrah, fetch drier logs;
Call Peter; he will show thee where they are.

SECOND FELLOW: I have a head, sir, that will find out logs,
And never trouble Peter for the matter.

CAPULET: Mass, and well said; a merry whoreson, ha!
Thou shalt be logger-head.

Exit Second Fellow

Good faith, 'tis day;
The County will be here with music straight,
For so he said he would.

Play Music

I hear him near.
Nurse! Wife! What, ho! What, nurse, I say!

Re-enter Nurse

Go waken Juliet, go and trim her up;
I'll go and chat with Paris. Hie, make haste,
Make haste. The bridegroom he is come already.
Make haste, I say.

Exeunt

SCENE V—*Juliet's chamber*

Enter Nurse

NURSE: Mistress! What, mistress! Juliet! Fast, I warrant her, she.
Why, lamb! Why, lady! Fie, you slug-a-bed!
Why, love, I say! madam! Sweetheart! Ehy, bride!
What, not a word? You take your pennyworths now.
Sleep for a week; for the next night, I warrant,
The County Paris hath set up his rest
That you shall rest but little. God forgive me!
Marry, and amen. How sound is she asleep!
I needs must wake her. Madam, madam, madam!
Ay, let the County take you in your bed;
He'll fright you up, i' faith. Will it not be?

Draws the curtains

What, dress'd, and in your clothes! and down again!
I must needs wake you. Lady! lady! lady!
Alas, alas! Help, help! my lady's dead!
O well-a-day that ever I was born!
Some aqua vitæ, ho! My lord! My lady!

Enter LADY CAPULET

LADY CAPULET: What noise is here?
NURSE: O lamentable day!
LADY CAPULET: What is the matter?
NURSE: Look, look! O heavy day!
LADY CAPULET: O me, O me! My child, my only life,
Revive, look up, or I will die with thee!
Help, help! Call help.

Enter CAPULET

CAPULET: For shame, bring Juliet forth; her lord is come.

NURSE: She's dead, deceased, she's dead; alack the day!
LADY CAPULET: Alack the day, she's dead, she's dead, she's dead!
CAPULET: Ha! let me see her. Out, alas! she's cold;
Her blood is settled, and her joints are stiff.
Life and these lips have long been separated.
Death lies on her like an untimely frost
Upon the sweetest flower of all the field.
NURSE: O lamentable day!
LADY CAPULET: O wœful time!
CAPULET: Death, that hath ta'en her hence to make me wail,
Ties up my tongue and will not let me speak.

Enter FRIAR LAWRENCE and PARIS, with Musicians

FRIAR LAWRENCE: Come, is the bride ready to go to church?
CAPULET: Ready to go, but never to return.
O son! the night before thy wedding day
Hath Death lain with thy wife. There she lies,
Flower as she was, deflowered by him.
Death is my son-in-law, Death is my heir;
My daughter he hath wedded; I will die,
And leave him all; life, living, all is Death's.
PARIS: Have I thought long to see this morning's face,
And doth it give me such a sight as this?
LADY CAPULET: Accursed, unhappy, wretched, hateful day!
Most miserable hour that e'er time saw
In lasting labour of his pilgrimage!
But one, poor one, one poor and loving child,
But one thing to rejoice and solace in,
And cruel Death hath catch'd it from my sight!
NURSE: O woe! O wœful, wœful, wœful day!
Most lamentable day, most wœful day,
That ever, ever, I did yet behold!
O day! O day! O day! O hateful day!

Never was seen so black a day as this.
O wœful day, O wœful day!

PARIS: Beguiled, divorced, wronged, spited, slain!
Most detestable Death, by thee beguil'd,
By cruel cruel thee quite overthrown!
O love! O life!—not life, but love in death!

CAPULET: Despised, distressed, hated, martyr'd, kill'd!—
Uncomfortable time, why camest thou now
To murder, murder our solemnity?
O child! O child! my soul, and not my child!
Dead art thou; alack! my child is dead,
And with my child my joys are buried.

FRIAR LAWRENCE: Peace, ho, for shame! Confusion's cure lives not
In these confusions. Heaven and yourself
Had part in this fair maid; now heaven hath all,
And all the better is it for the maid.
Your part in her you could not keep from death,
But heaven keeps his part in eternal life.
The most you sought was her promotion,
For 'twas your heaven she should be advanced;
And weep ye now, seeing she is advanced
Above the clouds, as high as heaven itself?
O, in this love, you love your child so ill
That you run mad, seeing that she is well.
She's not well married that lives married long,
But she's best married that dies married young.
Dry up your tears, and stick your rosemary
On this fair corse, and, as the custom is,
In all her best array bear her to church;
For though fond nature bids us an lament,
Yet nature's tears are reason's merriment.

CAPULET: All things that we ordained festival
Turn from their office to black funeral:
Our instruments to melancholy bells,
Our wedding cheer to a sad burial feast,
Our solemn hymns to sullen dirges change;
Our bridal flowers serve for a buried corse;
And all things change them to the contrary.
FRIAR LAWRENCE: Sir, go you in; and, madam, go with him;
And go, Sir Paris. Every one prepare
To follow this fair corse unto her grave.
The heavens do lour upon you for some ill;
Move them no more by crossing their high will.

Exeunt all bat Nurse and Musicians

FIRST MUSICIAN: Faith, we may put up our pipes and be gone.
NURSE: Honest good fellows, ah, put up, put up;
For well you know this is a pitiful case.

Exit

FIRST MUSICIAN: Ay, by my troth, the case may be amended.

Enter PETER

PETER: Musicians, O, musicians, 'Heart's ease, 'Heart's ease'! O, an you will have me live, play 'Heart's ease'.

FIRST MUSICIAN: Why 'Heart's ease'?

PETER: O, musicians, because my heart itself plays 'My heart is full of woe'. O, play me some merry dump to comfort me.

FIRST MUSICIAN: Not a dump we! 'Tis no time to play now.

PETER: You will not, then?

FIRST MUSICIAN: No.

PETER: I will then give it you soundly.

FIRST MUSICIAN: What will you give us?

PETER: No money, on my faith, but the gleek. I will give you the minstrel.

FIRST MUSICIAN: Then will I give you the serving-creature.

PETER: Then will I lay the serving-creature's dagger on your pate. I will carry no crotchets: I'll re you, I'll fa you; do you note me?

FIRST MUSICIAN: An you re us and fa us, you note us.

SECOND MUSICIAN: Pray you put up your dagger, and put out your wit.

PETER: Then have at you with my wit! I will dry-beat you with an iron wit, and put up my iron dagger. Answer me like men.

'When griping grief the heart doth wound
And doleful dumps the mind oppress,
Then music with her silver sound'—

Why 'silver sound'? Why 'music with her silver sound'? What say you, Simon Catling?

FIRST MUSICIAN: Marry, sir, because silver hath a sweet sound.

PETER: Pretty! What say you, Hugh Rebeck?

SECOND MUSICIAN: I say 'silver sound' because musicians sound for silver.

PETER: Pretty too! What say you, James Soundpost?

THIRD MUSICIAN: Faith, I know not what to say.

PETER: O, I cry you mercy, you are the singer; I will say for you. It is 'music with her silver sound' because musicians have no gold for sounding.

'Then music with her silver sound
With speedy help doth lend redress.'

Exit

FIRST MUSICIAN: What a pestilent knave is this same!

SECOND MUSICIAN: Hang him, Jack! Come, we'll in here; tarry for the mourners, and stay dinner.

Exeunt

Act V

Scene I—*Mantua: A street*

Enter ROMEO

ROMEO: If I may trust the flattering truth of sleep,
My dreams presage some joyful news at hand.
My bosom's lord sits lightly in his throne,
And all this day an unaccustom'd spirit
Lifts me above the ground with cheerful thoughts.
I dreamt my lady came and found me dead—
Strange dream, that gives a dead man leave to think!—
And breathed such life with kisses in my lips
That I revived, and was an emperor.
Ah me! how sweet is love itself possess'd,
When but love's shadows are so rich in joy!

Enter BALTHASAR, ROMEO's Man

News from Verona! How now, Balthasar!
Dost thou not bring me letters from the friar?
How doth my lady? Is my father well?
How fares my Juliet? that I ask again,
For nothing can be ill if she be well.

BALTHASAR: Then she is well, and nothing can be ill.
Her body sleeps in Capel's monument,
And her immortal part with angels lives.
I saw her laid low in her kindred's vault,
And presently took post to tell it you.
O, pardon me for bringing these ill news,

Since you did leave it for my office, sir.
ROMEO: Is it even so? Then I defy you, stars.
Thou know'st my lodging: get me ink and paper,
And hire post-horses; I will hence to-night.
BALTHASAR: I do beseech you, sir, have patience;
Your looks are pale and wild, and do import
Some misadventure.
ROMEO: Tush, thou art deceived;
Leave me, and do the thing I bid thee do.
Hast thou no letters to me from the friar?
BALTHASAR: No, my good lord.
ROMEO: No matter; get thee gone,
And hire those horses; I'll be with thee straight.

Exit BALTHASAR

Well, Juliet, I will lie with thee to-night.
Let's see for means. O mischief, thou art swift
To enter in the thoughts of desperate men!
I do remember an apothecary,
And hereabouts 'a dwells, which late I noted
In tatter'd weeds, with overwhelming brows,
Culling of simples. Meagre were his looks;
Sharp misery had worn him to the bones;
And in his needy shop a tortoise hung,
An alligator stuff'd, and other skins
Of ill-shaped fishes; and about his shelves
A beggarly account of empty boxes,
Green earthen pots, bladders, and musty seeds,
Remnants of packthread, and old cakes of roses,
Were thinly scatter'd, to make up a show.
Noting this penury, to myself I said
'An if a man did need a poison now,
Whose sale is present death in Mantua,

Here lives a caitiff wretch would sell it him'.
O, this same thought did but forerun my need;
And this same needy man must sell it me.
As I remember, this should be the house.
Being holiday, the beggar's shop is shut.
What, ho! Apothecary!

Enter Apothecary

APOTHECARY: Who calls so loud?

ROMEO: Come hither, man. I see that thou art poor.
Hold, there is forty ducats; let me have
A dram of poison, such soon-speeding gear
As will disperse itself through all the veins
That the life-weary taker may fall dead,
And that the trunk may be discharged of breath
As violently as hasty powder fired
Doth hurry from the fatal cannon's womb.

APOTHECARY: Such mortal drugs I have; but Mantua's law
Is death to any he that utters them.

ROMEO: Art thou so bare and full of wretchedness,
And fear'st to die? Famine is in thy cheeks,
Need and oppression starveth in thine eyes,
Contempt and beggary hangs upon thy back,
The world is not thy friend, nor the world's law;
The world affords no law to make thee rich;
Then be not poor, but break it and take this.

APOTHECARY: My poverty but not my will consents.

ROMEO: I pay thy poverty and not thy will.

APOTHECARY: Put this in any liquid thing you will.
And drink it off; and, if you had the strength
Of twenty men, it would dispatch you straight.

ROMEO: There is thy gold—worse poison to men's souls,
Doing more murder in this loathsome world
Than these poor compounds that thou mayst not sell.
I sell thee poison: thou hast sold me none.
Farewell; buy food, and get thyself in flesh.
Come, cordial and not poison, go with me
To Juliet's grave; for there must I use thee.

Exeunt

Scene II—*Friar Lawrence's cell*

Enter FRIAR JOHN

FRIAR JOHN: Holy Franciscan friar! brother, ho!

Enter FRIAR LAWRENCE

FRIAR LAWRENCE: This same should be the voice of Friar John.
Welcome from Mantua! What says Romeo?
Or, if his mind be writ, give me his letter.
FRIAR JOHN: Going to find a barefoot brother out,
One of our order, to associate me,
Here in this city visiting the sick,
And finding him, the searchers of the town,
Suspecting that we both were in a house
Where the infectious pestilence did reign,
Seal'd up the doors, and would not let us forth,
So that my speed to Mantua there was stay'd.
FRIAR LAWRENCE: Who bare my letter, then, to Romeo?
FRIAR JOHN: I could not send it—here it is again—
Nor get a messenger to bring it thee,
So fearful were they of infection.
FRIAR LAWRENCE: Unhappy fortune! By my brotherhood,
The letter was not nice, but full of charge

Of dear import; and the neglecting it
May do much danger. Friar John, go hence;
Get me an iron crow, and bring it straight
Unto my cell.

FRIAR JOHN: Brother, I'll go and bring it thee.

Exit

FRIAR LAWRENCE: Now must I to the monument alone.
Within this three hours will fair Juliet wake;
She will beshrew me much that Romeo
Hath had no notice of these accidents.
But I will write again to Mantua,
And keep her at my cell till Romeo come—
Poor living corse, closed in a dead man's tomb!

Exit

SCENE III—*Veron: A churchyard; in it the tomb of the Capulets*

Enter PARIS, and his Page bearing flowers and a torch

PARIS: Give me thy torch, boy; hence, and stand aloof;
Yet put it out, for I would not be seen.
Under yond yew trees lay thee all along,
Holding thy ear close to the hollow ground;
So shall no foot upon the churchyard tread—
Being loose, unfirm, with digging up of graves—
But thou shalt hear it. Whistle then to me,
As signal that thou hear'st something approach.
Give me those flowers. Do as I bid thee, go.

PAGE: [*Aside*] I am almost afraid to stand alone
Here in the churchyard; yet I will adventure.

Retires

PARIS: Sweet flower, with flowers thy bridal bed I strew—
O woe, thy canopy is dust and stones!—
Which with sweet water nightly I will dew;
Or, wanting that, with tears distill'd by moans.
The obsequies that I for thee will keep,
Nightly shall be to strew thy grave and weep.

The Page whistles

The boy gives warning something doth approach.
What cursed foot wanders this way to-night
To cross my obsequies and true love's rite?
What, with a torch! Muffle me, night, awhile.

Retires

Enter ROMEO and BALTHASAR, with a torch, a mattock, and a crow of Iron

ROMEO: Give me that mattock and the wrenching iron.
Hold, take this letter; early in the morning
See thou deliver it to my lord and father.
Give me the light; upon thy life I charge thee,
Whate'er thou hear'st or seest, stand all aloof
And do not interrupt me in my course.
Why I descend into this bed of death
Is partly to behold my lady's face,
But chiefly to take thence from her dead finger
A precious ring—a ring that I must use
In dear employment; therefore hence, be gone.
But if thou, jealous, dost return to pry
In what I further shall intend to do,
By heaven, I will tear thee joint by joint,
And strew this hungry churchyard with thy limbs.
The time and my intents are savage-wild,
More fierce and more inexorable far
Than empty tigers or the roaring sea.

BALTHASAR: I will be gone, sir, and not trouble ye.
ROMEO: So shalt thou show me friendship. Take thou that;
Live, and be prosperous: and farewell, good fellow.
BALTHASAR: [*Aside*] For all this same, I'll hide me hereabout;
His looks I fear, and his intents I doubt.

Retires

ROMEO: Thou detestable maw, thou womb of death,
Gorged with the dearest morsel of the earth,
Thus I enforce thy rotten jaws to open,

Breaking opens the tomb

And, in despite, I'll cram thee with more food.
PARIS: This is that banish'd haughty Montague
That murder'd my love's cousin—with which grief
It is supposed the fair creature died—
And here is come to do some villanous shame
To the dead bodies—I will apprehend him.
Stop thy unhallow'd toil, vile Montague.
Can vengeance be pursued further than death?
Condemned villain, I do apprehend thee.
Obey, and go with me; for thou must die.
ROMEO: I must indeed; and therefore came I hither.
Good gentle youth, tempt not a desperate man;
Fly hence, and leave me. Think upon these gone;
Let them affright thee. I beseech thee, youth,
Put not another sin upon my head
By urging me to fury; O, be gone!
By heaven, I love thee better than myself,
For I come hither arm'd against myself.
Stay not, be gone; live, and hereafter say
A madman's mercy bade thee run away.
PARIS: I do defy thy conjurations
And apprehend thee for a felon here.

ROMEO: Wilt thou provoke me? Then have at thee, boy!

They fight

PAGE: O lord, they fight! I will go call the watch.

Exit Paris falls

PARIS: O, I am slain! If thou be merciful,
Open the tomb, lay me with Juliet.

Dies

ROMEO: In faith, I will. Let me peruse this face.
Mercutio's kinsman, noble County Paris!
What said my man, when my betossed soul
Did not attend him as we rode? I think
He told me Paris should have married Juliet.
Said he not so, or did I dream it so?
Or am I mad, hearing him talk of Juliet,
To think it was so? O, give me thy hand,
One writ with me in sour misfortune's book!
I'll bury thee in a triumphant grave.
A grave? O no! A lantern, slaughter'd youth;
For here lies Juliet, and her beauty makes
This vault a feasting presence full of light.
Death, lie thou there, by a dead man interr'd.

Laying PARIS in the tomb

How oft when men are at the point of death
Have they been merry! Which their keepers call
A lightning before death. O, how may I
Call this a lightning? O my love! my wife!
Death, that hath suck'd the honey of thy breath,
Hath had no power yet upon thy beauty.
Thou art not conquer'd; beauty's ensign yet
Is crimson in thy lips and in thy cheeks,
And death's pale flag is not advanced there.

Tybalt, liest thou there in thy bloody sheet?
O, what more favour can I do to thee
Than with that hand that cut thy youth in twain
To sunder his that was thine enemy?
Forgive me, cousin. Ah, dear Juliet,
Why art thou yet so fair? Shall I believe
That unsubstantial Death is amorous,
And that the lean abhorred monster keeps
Thee here in dark to be his paramour?
For fear of that I still will stay with thee,
And never from this palace of dim night
Depart again. Here, here will I remain
With worms that are thy chambermaids. O, here
Will I set up my everlasting rest,
And shake the yoke of inauspicious stars
From this world-wearied flesh. Eyes, look your last.
Arms, take your last embrace. And, lips, O you
The doors of breath, seal with a righteous kiss
A dateless bargain to engrossing death!
Come, bitter conduct, come, unsavoury guide.
Thou desperate pilot, now at once run on
The dashing rocks thy sea-sick weary bark.
Here's to my love!

Drinks

O true apothecary!
Thy drugs are quick. Thus with a kiss I die.

Falls

Enter FRIAR LAWRENCE, with lantern, crow, and spade

FRIAR LAWRENCE: Saint Francis be my speed! How oft to-night
Have my old feet stumbled at graves! Who's there?

BALTHASAR: Here's one, a friend, and one that knows you well.

FRIAR LAWRENCE: Bliss be upon you! Tell me, good my friend,
What torch is yond that vainly lends his light
To grubs and eyeless skulls? As I discern,
It burneth in the Capel's monument.
BALTHASAR: It doth so, holy sir; and there's my master,
One that you love.
FRIAR LAWRENCE: Who is it?
BALTHASAR: Romeo.
FRIAR LAWRENCE: How long hath he been there?
BALTHASAR: Full half an hour.
FRIAR LAWRENCE: Go with me to the vault.
BALTHASAR: I dare not, sir.
My master knows not but I am gone hence,
And fearfully did menace me with death,
If I did stay to look on his intents.
FRIAR LAWRENCE: Stay, then, I'll go alone; fear comes upon me;
O, much I fear some ill unthrifty thing.
BALTHASAR: As I did sleep under this yew tree here,
I dreamt my master and another fought,
And that my master slew him.
FRIAR LAWRENCE: Romeo!
Alack, alack, what blood is this, which stains
The stony entrance of this sepulchre?
What mean these masterless and gory swords
To lie discolour'd by this place of peace?

Enters the tomb

Romeo! O, pale! Who else? What, Paris too?
And steep'd in blood? Ah, what an unkind hour
Is guilty of this lamentable chance!
The lady stirs.

JULIET wakes

JULIET: O comfortable friar! Where is my lord?
I do remember well where I should be,
And there I am. Where is my Romeo?

Noise within

FRIAR LAWRENCE: I hear some noise. Lady, come from that nest
Of death, contagion, and unnatural sleep;
A greater power than we can contradict
Hath thwarted our intents. Come, come away;
Thy husband in thy bosom there lies dead;
And Paris too. Come, I'll dispose of thee
Among a sisterhood of holy nuns.
Stay not to question, for the watch is coming;
Come, go, good Juliet, I dare no longer stay.
JULIET: Go, get thee hence, for I will not away.

Exit FRIAR LAWRENCE

What's here? A cup, closed in my true love's hand?
Poison, I see, hath been his timeless end.
O churl! drunk all, and left no friendly drop
To help me after? I will kiss thy lips;
Haply some poison yet doth hang on them,
To make me die with a restorative.

Kisses him

Thy lips are warm.
FIRST WATCHMAN: [*Within*] Lead, boy. Which way?
JULIET: Yea, noise? Then I'll be brief. O happy dagger!

Snatching ROMEO's dagger

This is thy sheath there rust, and let me die.

She Stabs herself Falls on ROMEO's body

Enter Watchman, with Paris's Page

PAGE: This is the place; there, where the torch doth burn.

FIRST WATCHMAN: The ground is bloody; search about the churchyard.

Go, some of you, whoe'er you find attach.

Exeunt some of the Watchman

Pitiful sight! here lies the County slain;
And Juliet bleeding, warm, and newly dead,
Who here hath lain these two days buried.
Go, tell the Prince; run to the Capulets;
Raise up the Montagues; some others search.

Exeunt others of the Watchman

We see the ground whereon these woes do lie;
But the true ground of all these piteous woes
We cannot without circumstance descry.

Re-enter some of the Watchman with BALTHASAR

SECOND WATCHMAN: Here's Romeo's man; we found him in the churchyard.

FIRST WATCHMAN: Hold him in safety till the Prince come hither.

Re-enter FRIAR LAWRENCE and another Watchman

THIRD WATCHMAN: Here is a friar that trembles, sighs, and weeps;

We took this mattock and this spade from him,
As he was coming from this churchyard side.

FIRST WATCHMAN: A great suspicion; stay the friar too.

Enter the PRINCE and Attendants

PRINCE: What misadventure is so early up,
That calls our person from our morning rest?

Enter CAPULET, LADY CAPULET, and Others

CAPULET: What should it be that they so shrieked abroad?

LADY CAPULET: The people in the street cry 'Romeo',

Some 'Juliet', and some 'Paris'; and all run,
With open outcry, toward our monument.

PRINCE: What fear is this which startles in our ears?

FIRST WATCHMAN: Sovereign, here lies the County Paris slain;
And Romeo dead; and Juliet, dead before,
Warm and new kill'd.

PRINCE: Search, seek, and know how this foul murder comes.

FIRST WATCHMAN: Here is a friar, and slaughter'd Romeo's man,
With instruments upon them fit to open
These dead men's tombs.

CAPULET: O heavens! O wife, look how our daughter bleeds!
This dagger hath mista'en, for, lo, his house
Is empty on the back of Montague,
And it mis-sheathed in my daughter's bosom.

LADY CAPULET: O me! this sight of death is as a bell
That warns my old age to a sepulchre.

Enter MONTAGUE and Others

PRINCE: Come, Montague, for thou art early up
To see thy son and heir more early down.

MONTAGUE: Alas, my liege, my wife is dead to-night;
Grief of my son's exile hath stopp'd her breath.
What further woe conspires against mine age?

PRINCE: Look, and thou shalt see.

MONTAGUE: O thou untaught! what manners is in this,
To press before thy father to a grave?

PRINCE: Seal up the mouth of outrage for a while,
Till we can clear these ambiguities,
And know their spring, their head, their true descent;
And then will I be general of your woes,
And lead you even to death. Meantime forbear,
And let mischance be slave to patience.

Bring forth the parties of suspicion.
FRIAR LAWRENCE: I am the greatest, able to do least,
Yet most suspected, as the time and place
Doth make against me, of this direful murder;
And here I stand, both to impeach and purge
Myself condemned and myself excused.
PRINCE: Then say at once what thou dost know in this.
FRIAR LAWRENCE: I will be brief, for my short date of breath
Is not so long as is a tedious tale.
Romeo, there dead, was husband to that Juliet;
And she, there dead, that Romeo's faithful wife.
I married them; and their stol'n marriage-day
Was Tybalt's doomsday, whose untimely death
Banish'd the new-made bridegroom from the city;
For whom, and not for Tybalt, Juliet pined.
You, to remove that siege of grief from her,
Betroth'd, and would have married her perforce,
To County Paris. Then comes she to me,
And with wild looks bid me devise some mean
To rid her from this second marriage,
Or in my cell there would she kill herself.
Then gave I her, so tutor'd by my art,
A sleeping potion; which so took effect
As I intended, for it wrought on her
The form of death. Meantime I writ to Romeo
That he should hither come as this dire night
To help to take her from her borrow'd grave,
Being the time the potion's force should cease.
But he which bore my letter, Friar John,
Was stay'd by accident, and yesternight
Return'd my letter back. Then all alone
At the prefixed hour of her waking

Came I to take her from her kindred's vault;
Meaning to keep her closely at my cell
Till I conveniently could send to Romeo.
But when I came, some minute ere the time
Of her awaking, here untimely lay
The noble Paris and true Romeo dead.
She wakes; and I entreated her come forth,
And bear this work of heaven with patience.
But then a noise did scare me from the tomb,
And she, too desperate, would not go with me,
But, as it seems, did violence on herself.
All this I know, and to the marriage
Her nurse is privy: and if aught in this
Miscarried by my fault, let my old life
Be sacrificed, some hour before his time,
Unto the rigour of severest law.
PRINCE: We still have known thee for a holy man.
Where's Romeo's man? what can he say in this?
BALTHASAR: I brought my master news of Juliet's death;
And then in post he came from Mantua
To this same place, to this same monument.
This letter he early bid me give his father;
And threatened me with death, going in the vault,
If departed not and left him there.
PRINCE: Give me the letter, I will look on it.
Where is the County's page, that raised the watch?
Sirrah, what made your master in this place?
PAGE: He came with flowers to strew his lady's grave;
And bid me stand aloof, and so I did.
Anon comes one with light to ope the tomb;
And by and by my master drew on him;
And then I ran away to call the watch.

PRINCE: This letter doth make good the friar's words,
Their course of love, the tidings of her death;
And here he writes that he did buy a poison
Of a poor pothecary, and therewithal
Came to this vault to die, and lie with Juliet.
Where be these enemies? Capulet, Montague,
See what a scourge is laid upon your hate,
That heaven finds means to kill your joys with love!
And I, for winking at your discords too,
Have lost a brace of kinsmen. All are punish'd.

CAPULET: O brother Montague, give me thy hand.
This is my daughter's jointure, for no more
Can I demand.

MONTAGUE: But I can give thee more;
For I will raise her statue in pure gold,
That while Verona by that name is known,
There shall no figure at such rate be set
As that of true and faithful Juliet.

CAPULET: As rich shall Romeo's by his lady's lie;
Poor sacrifices of our enmity!

PRINCE: A glooming peace this morning with it brings;
The sun for sorrow will not show his head.
Go hence, to have more talk of these sad things;
Some shall be pardon'd and some punished;
For never was a story of more woe
Than this of Juliet and her Romeo.

Exeunt

GLOSSARY

a': he
advanc'd: promoted
all along: at full length
ambling: elaborate walking
amerce: punish
and: if
antic face: grotesque mask
apace: quickly
aqua vitae: liquor, spirits
aspired: ascended to
associate: accompany
Aurora: the dawn

bankrout: bankrupt
behoveful: suitable
bent: intention
berlady: by Our Lady
bescreen'd: concealed
beskrew: bad luck to
blaze: make public
bosom's Lord: heart
bower: embower
buckler: small shield used with die long sword
by rote: by heart
caitiff: wretch
canker: maggot
canker'd : corrupted
chapters: without cheeks
charge: importance
checkring: variegating
chinks: cash
circumstance: knowledge of the facts
coil: confusion, fuss
commission: authority
conceit: imagination
consorted: allied
contract: bethrothal
cop'st: encounterest
count: reckoning
countervail: counterbalance
County: Count
crow: crowbar
crowkeeper: bird-scarer
cuWd: collected

deny: repudiate
discover: reveal
dislike: displease
division: melody, harmony
doublet: short coat
dump: doleful ditty
ensign: dag
fantasy: fancy
fay: faith
fearful: full of fear
fettle: make ready
fleckled: dappled

fleer: mock
fond: foolishly affectionate
frank: generous
full of charge: important directions
fume: mist

ghostly: spiritual
gleek: mocking retort
God shield: God prevent
green: fresh

hare: prostitute
harlotry: silly girl
hilding; worthless creature *humour:* (i) whim, (a) moisture
humorous: whimsical

indite: for invite

lace: cover with a pattern
lady-bird: sweetheart
level: aim
limits: boundaries

mammet: doll
manege: conduct
maw: stomach
measure: formal danoe
mew'd: caged
mickle: mighty
minion: hussy
modem: commonplace
mouse-hunt: wencher
move: discuss with
muffled: blindfold

natural: fool
needly: needfully
nice: trifling
nimble-pinioned: quick winged.

o'erperch: fly over
orisons: prayers
osier cage: wicker basket
owes: owns

passed: surpassed
passing: exceedingly
Phoebus: die sun
pitch: top ofthe flight of a hawk
pois'd: weighed
poor John: dried hake
portly: worthy
presently: immediately
pressed: weighed down
pride: point
princox: saucy boy
prodigious: ominous
prolixity: tedious excess

quit: reward

reeking: stinking
ropery: roguery
runagate: runaway
rushed: brushed

sadness: seriousness
season: keep flesh with salt

shield: forbid
shift: sacramental absolution following confession
smarter: prattle
sorted: chosen
sounded: swooned
sped: done for
spinner: spider
spleen: anger
stakes: fastens down
steads : benefits
still: always
stinted: stopped
stratagems: violent deeds
stuffed: full

teen: grief
tempering: allaying
tender: offer
tetchy: peevish
thought long: long desired
timeless: everlasting, untimely
Titan: the sun *toy:* trifle

uneven: indirect, unusual
unfurnished: unprovided
untainted: unbiassed
unthrifty: unlucky

validity: worth
vanished: escaped from
versal: universal
vestal: virgin

wanton: spoilt child
ward: minor, needing a guardian
washing: swashing, sweeping

'zounds: by God's wounds